Regression Healing I:
The Huntsman,
the Lord High Mayor
and the World War II Soldier

Wendy Rose Williams

D0150227

Body, Mind & Spirit/ Healing/ Energy
First Edition (December 2016)
First Printing (December 2016)

ISBN-10: 1539593703
ISNG-13: 978-1539593706

Formatting and "Map Man" Cover Design by LeiLani Doornbosch
Website: CustomCoverPro.com

PRAISE FOR "REGRESSION HEALING I: THE HUNTSMAN, THE LORD HIGH MAYOR AND THE WORLD WAR II SOLDIER"

"I wish you much success to introduce to the world that our biology is only temporary and our significance rests in our beautiful souls."
   Jill Rae Faulkner (Edina, Minnesota)

"An hour just flew by. I am loving your book – I feel like I'm on a journey with you two. I hope you do a huge series, because this is certainly a breath of fresh air!"
   Becky Buchko, Author
   (Johnstown, Pennsylvania)

"This is an incredible journey through past lives and into the great Light that is magnetic to all souls. These adventures give us a profound insight on how a lack of forgiveness can have a detrimental impact on this life and all future lifetimes. This book helps us know that there is indeed a great force in the Universe that is willing to work with us if we have a pure intention to assist others. The beautiful wisdom in the book gives a type of guidance that will benefit every entity alive. I am looking forward to Volume Two already!"

Chris Turner, Quantum Healing Centre (West Wellow, Hampshire, United Kingdom)

"This story is exceptionally well-written. It's a great book and I look forward to finishing it over the next few days. It's a very easy and interesting read. Well done!"

Heidi Unruh (Sherborn, Massachusetts)

"Wendy Williams works diligently to hold a pure space for her clients to delve deep into the consciousness of their own soul's treasures. This approach is fascinating! Her client account in 'Regression Healing I' is awesome, and touched me deeply. Enjoy the journey, and consider having your own session."

Robin Alexis, Author (Mt. Shasta, California)
RobinAlexis.com

"We need to see the good, the bad, and the ugly for us to learn. I would like to read more books in this series, with different healing processes (i.e., forgiveness in this book)."

Dr. Michael Tran (Manhattan, Kansas)

"I would absolutely read more of these books. It is almost like a series of Nancy Drew or the 'Mischievous Misadventures of Wendy Williams.' The book held my attention. When I started reading it today, my goal was to read half of it –

instead I couldn't put it down! I want an autographed copy."

Deborah Bonner, Past Life Regressionist (Stockbridge, Georgia)

"Overall an excellent book. Nice short read."

Ginger Beehler, Certified Life Coach & Psychic (Minnesota)

"I'm a big proponent of using a good, trustworthy Regressionist to assist in recalling past lives. It's helpful to not just recall them but to heal from any trauma associated and carried forward like extra baggage into this present life. This book does a great job of taking you along on the client's journey of remembering."

Laurie Regan, Author and Intuitive Artist (Seattle, Washington)

CONTENTS

DEDICATION

This book is dedicated to Dolores Cannon in recognition for her more than four decades of healing work, including creating the Quantum Healing Hypnotherapy technique (QHHT) and for her nineteen client session books.

My deep gratitude to Chris Turner, Dolores' student and creator of the Regression Healing technique, and to Irina Nola for introducing me to Chris.

I would also like to thank Dr. Michael Newton and his wife Peggy for their courageous, meticulous longitudinal reporting of more than seven thousand past-life regression and Life-Between-Lives client sessions detailed in "Journey of Souls" and "Destiny of Souls." Dr. Newton's work was my spiritual wake-up call in 2010 when I was led to "Journey of Souls" by the soul-mate who had the soul contract to "wake me up spiritually." Dr. Newton transitioned Home as I was completing this book. How fitting he chose September 21, "The International Day of Peace."

I'd like to extend my heartfelt appreciation to my fellow authors, beta readers, editors, proofreaders and other book cheerleaders, including Larry Cenotto, Chris Turner, LeiLani Doornbosch, Becky Buchko, Rich Vernadeau, Robin Alexis, Deborah Bonner, Linda Phelps, Ginger Beehler, Anthony Trimarchi, Michael Tran, Laurie Regan, Heidi Unruh, my mother Elizabeth Elliott, and more.

Thank you for the generous gifts of your time, energy, enthusiasm, and expertise provided. LeiLani not only designed the perfect book cover in the blink of an eye, but provided knowledgeable technical publishing advice. Heather Molina assisted with key word selection, and Jason Havey and others provided a forum for me to speak publicly about quantum healing, including the need for and amazing power of forgiveness.

My immense gratitude to the many friends and healers who helped me surmount significant writing and publishing blocks, including Robin Alexis, Jude Ponton, Matthew Bueno, Darcy Pariso, Laurie Regan, Larry Cenotto, Irina Nola, Chris Turner, Angela Pate, and others. You helped me move into my life purpose and soul mission more than you know.

May you and all readers be blessed with abundant peace, love and joy – the Heaven on Earth energies!

AUTHOR'S NOTE

I was introduced to Past Life Regression and Life-Between-Lives via Dr. Michael Newton's best-selling "Journey of Souls." I had my own first Past-Life Regression session as the client in 2011 and was astonished by the healing benefits during a mere two hours. My lifetime of anxiety was healed.

I became intrigued by Dr. Brian Weiss' work with regression clients, Dick Sutphen's soul-mate books, Dr. Helen Wambach's pioneering research, and Dolores Cannon's Quantum Healing Hypnotherapy Technique. Over the next few years as I did my own informal research including a plethora of reading, I also had many healing sessions and countless energetic and spiritual experiences.

My conclusion is that our souls are eternal and that we reincarnate many times to learn carefully chosen lessons. I believe the soul craves experiences, above all else, in order to have the opportunity to progress. Some of these experiences such as abuse or war are incomprehensible when viewed from the lens of a single human incarnation – one has to pull up to the soul-level to understand their greater purpose. Regression Healing provides clients the opportunity to tap into the wisdom of their souls without requiring they have special abilities or training.

My belief is emotions are timeless and are stored at the soul level. Some trapped emotions may present physically, emotionally or mentally as distress or disease to provide us with the opportunity to heal and release them. This allows us to enhance both our present and future incarnations.

I began formally training as a healer -- including as a Past Life Regressionist -- to be able to offer others the multitude of breakthroughs I've experienced via various healing techniques. I chose Regression Healing – inspired by Dolores Cannon's Quantum Healing Hypnotherapy Technique – for its versatility, effectiveness, ease, beauty and power.

Regression Healing can address a wide variety of issues ranging from anxiety, depression, PTSD, anger, chronic pain, many disorders or diseases, and more. Clients can receive great clarity as to their life purpose and their larger soul mission, and learn how to enhance their health, wealth, and relationships as we leave the past in the past, and fully embrace NOW.

A friend I'd known in many lives found it difficult to connect with his Spirit Guides. He had severe neck, shoulder, back, kidney and knee pain from his lifetime as an athlete and adventurer. We agreed to do a Regression Healing session in the fall of 2015 to request healing and important information to enhance his current life. I chose to call him "Simon" in this book to protect his privacy and that of his loved ones. I chose the name Simon as one of its translations is "He who listens to God."

Within a few days of scheduling with Simon, I was surprised to hear from Spirit that this would be "the most difficult session of my lifetime." I couldn't get more information other than it was extremely important for both of us to proceed. I anticipated the issue was Simon is highly intelligent and left-brained, meaning although he's done previous work with Past-Life Regressions and other spiritual journeying, it's difficult for him to reach and remain at a therapeutic level of trance as he questions during the process versus visioning and journeying.

I expected a fair bit of "wrestling" to help Simon allow his ego, or left-brain, to relax and enjoy the ride. Our goal was to bring forth healing and releasing of old energies that no longer served him, and to request answers to some of his important questions.

What occurred during this session instead became the ultimate lesson in forgiveness. Simon had to forgive others for what many would consider unforgivable acts in his past lives in order to heal his body and spirit now.

We had to forgive each other, too, in a profound and unexpected way. I then had to take the final step and forgive myself to be willing to share this story publicly.

My practice is to record all sessions, in order to provide the client with an MP3 audio file to work with after his or her session. This allows clients to continue healing at a deeper level. Much of the information from a Regression Healing session can be immediately forgotten if it's not written down or recorded in some manner, though everything is stored at both the soul level and in the Akashic Records and can be accessed if necessary.

I felt strongly guided to record Simon's session with two devices, which was unusual. Why would I need two? But the message was clear, so I followed it. I used both my new MP3 recorder and my iPhone. My MP3 recorder had fresh batteries, and works perfectly. We tested it that morning as we began Simon's session. I placed the MP3 recorder directly next to him, on the far side away from me. I could see the red light was on and remained on during the four-plus hours we journeyed. I then started my phone recorder and placed it between us where I could see the timer was running fine on my phone, too. Neither turned off during his session or needed the recording restarted.

Yet when I went to transfer the file from my MP3 recorder to Simon's laptop after his session, nothing was audible! Not a single word. This never happened with my MP3 recorder before or since. There was nothing to hear from his more than four-hour session beyond the separate "Testing, Testing 123" recording we'd made with the date and our names at the start of session. Yet the small red recording light had clearly been on the entire time. We both had seen it.

I sensed energetic interference. But why? I took a deep breath, prayed, cleared my energy, and checked my phone recording. Fortunately, I could hear both of us as clear as day on my new iPhone voice recorder. The file was extremely large, so I wasn't able to transfer it immediately from my phone to Simon's laptop as he didn't have Dropbox installed, which is the utility I use to move large files. We agreed I'd send him the MP3 later that day from my phone.

But the file wouldn't transfer from my phone once I tried to send it from home that evening. It felt "sticky" somehow, like it belonged with me. I had sent large MP3 to clients easily before from my phone, so had assumed it would be easier with a new phone. Customer Service wasn't able to help me when I called, so I went to the store in-person the next day. They were unable to move the file from my phone either, and theorized the MP3 was simply too large.

I wasn't able to give up my phone to Simon for long enough for him to listen to his session on his own. Yet I knew it was vital he have the information in all its detail as he'd had a powerful session, and I knew from our quick debrief afterwards that he only recalled portions of it. He estimated the session length at around two to two and a half hours, when it had actually been about four and a half hours. This is one of the hallmarks of a highly successful session, for the client to underestimate the time. He couldn't recall much of what he'd stated while in the theta level as his Higher Self, Guides and the Light, which was why he really needed his recording. Or a transcript...

I gritted my teeth and began typing what I knew from experience would be a time-consuming document. I estimated fifty to sixty pages or more. I typed for about three hours the first day of transcription before taking a break. I quickly skimmed what I'd typed. I was shocked to discover what I planned as a straightforward transcript with our two names in rotation and what we'd each said instead had a title page and my name as the author? There was also a note to add this Author's Note, a Table of Contents, and a place for a Forgiveness Resource Guide at the end.

This was a BOOK? A book to be shared publicly? That was not my intent when I began typing Simon's session transcript. The content felt raw and uniquely personal, so I pushed that possibility aside. Otherwise I knew I would likely block the cathartic journey I sensed we were on. I blessed my mother Elizabeth for the millionth time for encouraging me to take typing class in eighth grade.

I carefully transcribed what became the heart of this book. Dialog has been smoothed in places to make it flow more readily. Additional background was provided where beta readers recommended it, particularly in the area of our shared past lives. They weren't spelled out in any detail by Simon during the session as we both already knew what had transpired in our past lives together, but the reader would not. Some additional dialog was added for teaching purposes.

This book contains tremendous healing for both of us as we closed out old energies and mastered our final lesson – forgiveness, and parting peacefully. Forgiveness doesn't always come easily. Self-forgiveness is often the most difficult journey of all. The consequences of not forgiving or learning another key lesson can be far-reaching, including into many if not all of our future lives if we don't fully master a lesson. The learning opportunity will then present again, and often in a larger way, until we master it. Karma and soul contracts can be used as soul-level teaching tools and techniques.

I emailed the word document to Simon the moment it was transcribed so I wouldn't second-guess my decision. I released the outcome, and asked him if he would consider sharing it publicly with his identity and that of his family and friends blinded, but with me identified. I prayed he would say yes – I prayed even more he'd say no!

Yet it was time for me to step to the plate with our story, with Simon's permission. It was time for me to "Cast My Call Loudly" as my friend Jason Havey shared with me as a message from the Light at the end of Jason's own Regression Healing session a few months later.

I knew Simon's comprehensive session could help others who wanted to understand how a Past Life Regression session could improve their lives *now*, and what a Regression Healing session is really like, though all sessions are unique. It's also a terrific illustration of our own journey to learn to forgive at the deepest level. If you don't forgive, you will keep meeting each other in remarkable ways or someone else will bring the lesson home in a larger and more dramatic way.

Simon agreed immediately his story was meant to be publicly shared in its entirety. I then teetered sharply back and forth between happiness and horror. I needed to complete my own journey to self-forgiveness to be willing to share his session as it's so personal to me. Most Regression Healing sessions don't include any shared past lives between the client and the Past-Life Regressionist as there aren't any, or they're not pertinent to what the client most needs to heal or to learn as determined by their Higher Self, Guides and the Light. In other cases there is an excellent reason for a client to choose a particular Past-Life Regressionist, or for the Regressionist to offer a session to a client as I did in order for both to heal and release old energies that no longer serve them.

My intent in sharing this small portion of our soul-mate journey is to inspire others how to untangle complex energies when you've lived many lives with another soul. Simon and I found 16 shared lives. We're not in the same primary soul group, but I did find him and his mother in an adjacent group during my own four-hour Life-Between-Lives spiritual regression with Dr. Dominique Glaub, a Dr. Michael Newton therapist in Seattle, Washington.

There is much confusion on the topic of "soul-mates." Many want a soul-mate to be the love of their life, a fabulous hot romance like no other, and one that lasts a lifetime. I shared that highly romantic expectation when Simon and I first met again this life.

I've since learned – re-remembered, more accurately – soul-mates are for LESSONS. We can apply that learning to progress at the soul level. Some lessons are easy and joyful. Other lessons can be incredibly challenging and can span many lifetimes, which is why we choose someone with whom we work extremely well to master an area.

Like many soul-mates, Simon and I have been best friends of the same and different genders; we've been mother and son; he may have been my domineering older brother; we've served in the silent monasteries multiple times as scribes; he was a young brave in my tribe when I was a Medicine Woman; we were sacred sexuality partners; we married in six different lifetimes including several writer past lives; we've been infamous North Seas pirates; he was the Sea Captain that brought my family safely to Colonial America; and in another life with me he was again a Sea Captain. That time we married and had a large family, and it appears I was involved with the Underground Railroad.

I've had to endure the horror of seeing him beheaded and to witness him drown without being able to save his life. He buried me on our farm at the base of our favorite tree in the days before cemeteries. We were philanthropists who served mankind with great joy, and I found it very hard to accept that we weren't going to do so again together this lifetime. We betrayed each other as King and Queen and he had me imprisoned in a nunnery for many decades. He lied to me and abandoned me, and has been my greatest fan. I've both tortured and healed him. We've broken each other's hearts profoundly many times, and we've loved and supported each other without question for thousands of years.

This is a soul-mate connection. Soul-mates can typically recognize the other's unique energetic signature at some level. I recognized his carriage, his voice, and his strong, easy confidence at our first meeting – our reunion – in this lifetime. He seemed to recognize my eyes and something about the shape of my face. As you will read in this Regression Healing session, he knows my energy regardless of the lifetime, my appearance, gender, the context, or the timing.

We were not able to sustain our romance long-term in this lifetime. What became more crucial was to transmute our karma – our unbalanced energies – to fulfill our shared soul contracts and to transmute those that no longer served us, and to raise our vibrational levels. We both needed to heal our hearts, our bodies, our emotions and our souls. We had to forgive one another fully to part peacefully.

I extend my deepest gratitude to the man who allowed me to share his session publicly without hesitation, and for modeling forgiveness so graciously. Bless you for spiritually waking me up in this lifetime. Thank you for inspiring me to step into my power fully, without abusing it, including not only to write, but to publicly share my spiritual essence once again without fear. You encouraged me countless times that if I let go of "what will other people think," I would be free to live my destiny that has been written in the stars.

Wendy Rose Williams
September 21, 2016
The International Day of Peace

I: THE HUNTSMAN

(Note: Simon's four-and-a-half-hour session has been underway for 46 minutes. A boat was used to travel to a location which "will provide healing or contain important knowledge for you today." Possibilities include a past life, earlier in the current lifetime, as a non-human energy form, in a different dimension or on another planet, for example.

Wendy built suggestions slowly and with strong, repetitive detail, as Simon had expressed difficulty in reaching and then maintaining a sufficient level of trance in previous sessions with other practitioners. He didn't meditate or relax easily, but was extremely visual, observant, and adept at visioning as an athlete, so she planned to use those natural abilities. Plus he had done similar work previously on at least three occasions, and there is a learning curve to attaining a therapeutic level of trance.)

Wendy *(Past-Life Regressionist)*: Are you coming off the boat yet?

Simon *(Client)*: I just sort of exited - I went to a cliff edge above the river - I came up to a big rounded cliff edge, like a place in Yosemite?

Wendy: Excellent. What else do you see around you?

Simon: Just a lot of forest.

Wendy: Okay - look down – what does it look--

(He interrupts, a good sign seeing images clearly.)

Simon: It looks like a medieval town in the distance!

Wendy: Very good - look down – are you wearing anything on your feet?

Simon: *(sounding a little concerned)* I don't see them clearly.

Wendy: *(reassuringly)* That's fine. Things will become clearer as we go along.

Does your body feel male or female?

Simon: Male.

Wendy: Does your body feel healthy?

Simon: Yes.

Wendy: Are you carrying anything as you observe those cliffs and the forest and see the town in the distance?

Simon: Arrows, it seems like.

Wendy: Arrows. Okay. You're carrying arrows. Do you feel like you belong there?

Simon: *(hesitating)* I'm comfortable there...

(pause)

Wendy: But? You sound like you want to say more.

2

Simon: I don't know if I belong there.

Wendy: So you're comfortable there. Do you feel young or old?

Simon: I definitely don't feel old - I don't know if I'm young, though.

Wendy: That's fine. You're doing really well. Look down – what are you wearing on your feet? You can see your feet clearly now.

Simon: Oh! Right. I see some sort of high-ankle deerskin things.

Wendy: Very good. What color are they?

Simon: Deep brown.

Wendy: What are you wearing on the rest of your body?

Simon: Like a wool cloak thing, and tight britches.

Wendy: You're doing great. What color is the cloak?

Simon: A grey-brown.

Wendy: Very good. Look down again - what does the ground look like that you're standing on – what's it comprised of?

Simon: A lot of leaves – kind of marshy.

(pause)

Simon: No, not marshy, kind of wet. Some grasses...

Wendy: Okay, some grasses, and it's kind of wet. Look at your wrists and fingers – are you wearing anything there, or around your neck?

Simon: On my right wrist there's this thing like a bowman would wear – I think it prevents the arrow from slicing across your arm? I don't know what it's called.

3

Wendy: You're communicating really well – I'm following you easily. We don't have to know the exact word. Look more carefully at what you're carrying. What is it?

Simon: Very little.

(Pause as she formulated her next question to see if he'd say more about the arrows, without her suggesting it.)

Wendy: Do you have anything slung over either shoulder or across your back?

Simon: It's kind of like an oil...

(pause)

Simon: *(hesitating)* A small oil sack?

Wendy: Okay. What's inside the oil sack?

Simon: I don't know. I can't see inside.

(pause)

Simon: It seems like food, maybe.

Wendy: Perfect. What else do you see around you?

Simon: Rocks. Some farms in the distance below.

Wendy: So where are you going?

Simon: Into town.

Wendy: Excellent. Let's go into town!

Wendy: Is there anyone with you as you head into town?

Simon: No.

Wendy: How do you feel?

Simon: *(cheerfully)* Light!

Wendy: *(smiling as he was so happy)* Wonderful! Let's proceed into town. What do you see as you arrive?

Simon: Cattle. Women in frocks. Lots of posts. Smoke coming up from the chimneys.

Wendy: Fantastic, that's so descriptive.

(pause)

Wendy: What are the posts for?

Simon: Fences, and to tether horses.

Wendy: Okay – to tie horses to – you're seeing very clearly now. What is the year?

(She chose to ask Simon the year which some Past Life Regressionists don't do as they feel it takes the client back into their left brain as numbers are stored there, and they need to vision from their right brain. But he was visioning strongly at that moment, so she chose to ask him, as the year can be quite informative.)

Simon: The number 1883 flashes for me.

Wendy: Wonderful! Great job! What's your name?

Simon: I don't have any clarity on that – there are too many names flashing for me all at once. I can't catch them fast enough.

Wendy: That's okay. What do you see as you go into town and see the posts, and the women in their frocks in 1883... what happens next?

Simon: I seem out of place. I feel light and free, but I feel out of place.

Wendy: So this might not be where you live, but rather somewhere you're visiting?

Simon: Oh, I'm sure I don't live there.

Wendy: Okay. Got it.

(Pauses to consider whether to direct Simon in this past life, or to give him a choice. As he was visioning clearly at that point she chose to give him a choice. Otherwise she would have directed him more strongly to help him vision more easily.)

Wendy: Would you like to explore the town further, or to go to the place you live?

Simon: The place I live.

Wendy: Very good. Let's go NOW to the place where you live.

I would like you to go to where you live, and look at the outside of it...

Simon: It's sort of small – chalet-like, with a sod roof.

Wendy: Excellent description. What else?

Simon: There's a little balcony.

Wendy: How do you enter your chalet?

Simon: On the bottom floor. There's like an open door – it's the level where the animals are kept.

Wendy: *(confused)* Pardon me? The animals?

(Pause as she formulates her next question, not having expected this description.)

Wendy: Go inside and describe to me the details of what you see.

What types of animals do you see on that ground level?

Simon: *(slowly)* I see a dog, I see at least 2 horses, and I can't tell if those are – uhhh – sheep or cattle?

Wendy: You're doing great! Go upstairs – how do you get upstairs – is there an internal or an external staircase?

Simon: Internal staircase, going from where the animals are inside.

Wendy: Go upstairs and take a look around. You'll be able to see very clearly what your home looks like. What do you see?

Simon: I see a view over some short trees.

Wendy: How many windows are there?

Simon: Can't tell. It seems like a big plate-glass window, but that's not realistic...

Simon: *(sounding frustrated)* It's just a big open view...

Wendy: You're doing very well. You don't need to analyze it now, you'll be able to do that later. You're extremely bright and quite visual. Just vision it. What else do you see in that room? I know you're seeing a lot. You can do this work extremely well. Focus on what you DO see or sense. What can you see?

Simon: A handmade bench...

Wendy: Okay, go take a closer look at it.

Simon: A counter – a dark burled table, some stools.

Wendy: Excellent! How do you prepare your food? Do you cook inside or outside?

Simon: I don't really see any kitchen prep.

Wendy: That's okay. What's your favorite place in your home? I'd like you to go there – where's your favorite spot?

Simon: A big chair of some sort in the corner.

Wendy: Wonderful. What's by the chair? What does the big chair look like?

7

Simon: There's an oil lamp of some sort, and a table.

Wendy: What do you like—

Simon: *(interrupts excitedly)* I see a big, big chair – it's so clear now – it's made for one!

Wendy: *(smiling)* Excellent. What do you like to do when you sit in that chair, that favorite spot in your house?

Simon: *(pause while he considers)* I like to read here, and to sleep.

Wendy: What are some of your favorite things to read?

Simon: Biographies, poetry, a little bit of history, I think.

Wendy: Where are you living? Do you have a sense of a city or town, where you're located geographically?

Simon: It's not in a city or even a town – it's not even in the outskirts.

Wendy: Okay. So a remote location.

Simon: Isolated.

Wendy: Do you have a sense where this isolated place is?

Simon: No.

Wendy: Okay. Does anyone live with you in your home?

Simon: I don't think so. I don't get that impression.

Wendy: Do you see any other rooms, or is it essentially one big room?

Simon: It seems to be one big room.

Wendy: *(calmly)* So it's one big room. Now see yourself eating a meal. Can you sit down at your table or where you normally eat, and describe what you see on the table.

(long pause)

Simon: I see a rabbit.

Wendy: Very good! How did you prepare your rabbit?

Simon: *(hesitating)* I think it was cooked over a spit?

Wendy: You're doing great! Do you have anything else with the rabbit?

Simon: Some sort of greens – I can't say what they are.

Wendy: You're doing fantastic. What do you drink with your meal – do you have anything to drink with your rabbit and greens?

Simon: *(pause)* Hmmm. Water and beer come to mind.

Wendy: Wonderful! Trust your first impression, you're doing super. What do you do for a living?

Simon: I don't know – I seem to be a hunter.

Wendy: SEE yourself doing it – is that what you're doing – hunting?

Simon: I'm traveling a lot. A lot of walking.

Wendy: Are you tracking?

Simon: I don't seem to be doing that much hunting.

Wendy: Are you tracking when you're walking?

Simon: No, I don't seem to be tracking.

Wendy: What do you do with the majority of your time, in addition to walking, hunting, and time at home?

Simon: *(pause)* I don't know. A lot of walking.

Wendy: Ok, lots of walking. Do you ever see any people?

(long pause)

Simon: One face comes to mind – I apparently visit this old man often. Beyond that, I don't know.

Wendy: *(cheerfully)* Wonderful, we can go visit this old man! Would you like to do that?

Simon: Yes.

Wendy: Does the old man live near your home, or do you have to walk a distance to get to him?

Simon: No, he's in town. I have to walk a distance to get to him.

Wendy: Go there NOW. What does his place look like?

Simon: His place is very dark.

Wendy: Okay, it's dark inside. What do you do when you visit him? Do you bring him anything? Look down at your hands. You can see very well now.

Simon: Oh! I see it now. I've got food. I bring him food, I think. And I listen to him a lot.

Wendy: What does he have to tell you? We can hear him very clearly now – what does he have to tell you?

Simon: He tells me the way things are, and the way things were. He tells me what works. How things clip together.

Wendy: Do you consider him a mentor of sorts?

Simon: Very clearly, yes.

Wendy: Okay. What does he call you? You can clearly hear him greet you by name when you arrive.

Simon: Manfred comes to mind.

Wendy: Excellent. Hello, Manfred. Is the old man a relative?

Simon: *(as his past life self, Manfred)* I don't think so. I don't get that impression.

Wendy: Is he in your life now? You'll recognize him easily if he is.

Manfred: *(pause)* I think he is.

Wendy: Who is he now?

Manfred: Ummm...my buddy *(name deleted)* who lives down in *(location deleted)*.

Wendy: Oh, wonderful! You're doing so well. Do you enjoy visiting him, or does it more feel like duty or necessity?

Manfred: We seem to have a lot in common.

Wendy: *(nodding)* Great. What is the weather like on those many long walks when you go see your friend in town?

(no reply)

Wendy: What is the weather like? Does it...

Manfred: I don't see a lot of gloom or rain or snow.

Wendy: Okay – does it get extremely hot?

Manfred: No, I don't think so.

Wendy: So it sounds fairly temperate. Nice. Is there anything more you can learn from that time and that place?

Manfred: Yes. I want to summarize. *(lecturing her a bit)* We're supposed to summarize, you know.

(She smiled, knowing he needed to feel comfortable he was controlling his own experience.)

Wendy: Perfect. What was your life as Manfred about?

Manfred: There was a lot of learning – I feel very free, very independent. I'm coming and going at will. Not having a lot of obligations.

Wendy: Is that a feeling you'd like more of now?

Simon: *(shifting back to his current life persona)* I have plenty of that now.

Wendy: *(clarifying)* You have plenty of obligations now, or plenty of freedom?

Simon: Plenty of freedom.

Wendy: Excellent. What more --

Simon: *(interrupting)* It was like setting the bar – the tempo – the template...

(tapering off)

Wendy: Were you setting the template that lifetime for your current life?

Simon: For many lifetimes. It seems like setting it for a number of lifetimes.

Wendy: Wonderful. Is there anything else you'd like to observe from that lifetime?

(Simon switches back to speaking as Manfred. He shifts about a bit, and phrases his comment delicately.)

Manfred: Ummm – I seem to be totally separated from any – any like – ummmm – female companionship, or notions of romance. I'm wondering about that.

Wendy: How does that make you feel?

Manfred: More curious, than anything.

Wendy: You're able to explore this. Was this part of a life lesson, or just how your life as Manfred worked out? What was the reason? There's a reason you're being shown this information.

Simon: That life, you mean?

Wendy: Yes. That life, as well as your observation there doesn't seem to be any female companionship.

Simon: It seems to be the genus of being a cause, instead of an effect – like determining your own path. Not being able to put it down on you as duty – it just seems very freeing.

Wendy: Is that what was most important to you, that feeling of freedom?

Simon: It's the overwhelming sense of that lifetime.

Wendy: Excellent! You're really putting the pieces together well.

(pause)

Wendy: Do you feel there's anything more you can learn from that time and place?

Simon: I always – even in an atmosphere of freedom – look at how to fit and contribute to a greater whole – I don't see in this lifetime how that is done, but the awareness is there.

Wendy: The awareness is there because when you first arrived there you felt out-of-place, and now you're starting to feel pieces of the puzzle come in?

Simon: I felt out-of-place then coming into town, not out-of-place, period.

Wendy: Thank you for clarifying. What else?

Simon: I think there were people I fit with – I've only seen one, but in my other Past Life Regressions and Life-Between-Lives, there's been the presence of women – here the energy doesn't come up at all.

Wendy: I understand. Each life experience can be very unique and different. Just stay with the time and place where you're Manfred, please. You don't need to analyze one life vis-à-vis another right now.

(pause)

Wendy: Is there anything more you can learn from that time and place?

(no reply)

Wendy: Is there something to explore there further?

Manfred: I'd like to see why I seem to be so far behind the times.

Wendy: *(frowning, noting the energy level falling)* What do you mean "behind the times?"

Simon: *(sounding frustrated)* Well, 1883 came up, and I seem to be living the life of William Tell in the 1500s vs. 1883! I seem to be living a knife-and-plate existence versus the refinement that would be in place in 1883.

Wendy: Let's explore with the images, and not over-engage our left brain trying to figure it out. Let your profound knowledge of history go, just for the moment. You are extremely capable of this work –

you are doing great! You are a lifetime athlete – you know how to visualize very powerfully.

(pause)

Wendy: *(crisply)* What is the answer to why you chose that lifetime? Why is it the way it is? Why are we being shown this one? You know the answer – just look within yourself. All the answers are there.

(Long pause as energy builds and Simon moves back to experiencing being Manfred.)

Manfred: It seems to me it's to show that you can set the bar yourself.

Wendy: Yes. What else?

Manfred: You can order up your own circumstances.

Wendy: That's a great insight. And?

(long pause)

Wendy: Do you feel there's anything more you can learn from that time and place?

Manfred: It's not coming to me right now.

Wendy: That's fine. This is really strong work.

(brief pause – switches gears to move him to another scene)

Wendy: Now that you have an understanding of why you were shown this time and place...

(She moves him to the next scene that will "contain healing or important information for his life now." No other instructions are given so that he is free to choose without being influenced by suggestions from her.)

II: THE LORD HIGH MAYOR

Wendy: You can see very clearly now. What's the first thing you see?

Simon *(speaking as new past life persona)*: A really ornate stone – it's carved stone – it's on the corner of a building. It must be a church or cathedral?

Wendy: You're doing great! What else do you see or sense there?

Simon: Lots of height – lots of little capstones – lots of arches. I'm only seeing the corner, though. It's very involved.

Wendy: So carry on your natural course. What are you doing there?

Simon: I have a cloak on of some sort – I'm some sort of nobleman or official?

Wendy: You're doing great! What color is your cloak?

Nobleman: It's a reddish-black.

Wendy: Very good. Look down at your feet. What are you wearing on your feet?

Nobleman: Pointy shoes.

Wendy: Pointy shoes. What color?

Nobleman: Green.

(She had to suppress a snicker at the thought of Simon in pointy green shoes as it made her think of him as an elf.)

Wendy: What condition are they in? Well-maintained or –

(He interrupted, sounding formal, even a bit haughty, as he more became that past life character.)

Nobleman: I assure you, Madame, my shoes are in very good condition! They are not muddy, they are not worn...

Wendy: *(respectfully)* I understand. What are you wearing besides your cloak and the green shoes?

Nobleman: Lots of black.

Wendy: Lots of black. Are you male or female?

Nobleman: Male.

Wendy: How old are you?

Nobleman: Middle-aged.

Wendy: Does your body feel healthy?

(pause)

Nobleman: It feels heavy.

Wendy: *(puzzled)* It feels heavy?

(pause as she formulates her next question)

Wendy: Why do you feel heavy?

Nobleman: I don't feel spritely. I have some girth to me.

Wendy: *(nodding)* Oh, I see. Thank you for helping me understand that better. Are you wearing anything around your neck, on your fingers or wrists?

Nobleman: *(thoughtfully)* I've got bad teeth.

(Doesn't think to ask if his teeth or mouth need healing, which would have been ideal. Pause as she formulates her next question as dental health makes her curious about the year.)

Wendy: You see you have bad teeth. What year is it?

(long pause; energy feels unsettled)

Nobleman: The year is not clear. 1266 keeps coming up. I keep fighting it!

Wendy: Please go with your first impression – it's the right one. Great job, it feels like 1266.

(See Author's End Note with possible thread between the year 1266 in the second life, the name Manfred in the first life, and the upcoming third life.)

Wendy: Please tune into the geography when you're the Nobleman wearing the red-black cape. Where are you?

(pause)

Nobleman: France, I think.

Wendy: France. Very good. You have an excellent sense of time and place. Would you like to explore inside the Cathedral, or to go to the place you live?

Nobleman: The place I live.

Wendy: Excellent. Go there NOW! Know you can see the outside in very clear detail, and it will be easy to describe to me. What does it look like?

Nobleman: Big, square-cut stones. Mossy. Vines crawling up the sides...

(pause)

Wendy: Yes? What else do you see? You're seeing a lot.

Nobleman: It doesn't seem to be ideally maintained. It's a chateau-style that has been in the family for a long time, and I've inherited it. It's big, and not particularly in good shape – I've got other things on my mind – maintaining the house is not one of them.

Wendy: That's fine. Let's go inside – how do you enter your home?

Nobleman: The door on the bottom level.

Wendy: Okay. What is on your mind – what do you spend most of your time doing?

Nobleman: Some sort of civic duty.

Wendy: See yourself doing it – who's involved? What do you do?

Nobleman: *(chuckling, looking very happy)* I meet with everybody, it seems like.

Wendy: So lots of people to meet with. Are they city officials, or...?

Nobleman: Military officials, city officials, everybody. Lots and lots of people and meetings.

Wendy: How do you feel about what you described as your civic duty?

Nobleman: It feels very satisfying.

Wendy: Fantastic! So it feels very satisfying. What is your role – are you getting different groups to come together? What is the purpose?

Nobleman: I make sure things run smoothly. I'm very competent at what I do, and I keep competing interests well-oiled, lubricated, out of conflict with each other.

Wendy: And who –

19

Nobleman: *(interrupting excitedly)* Like I'm some sort of ombudsman, but more important than that.

Wendy: Who does your work benefit?

Nobleman: The city.

Wendy: Okay. How so?

Nobleman: My work keeps things running smoothly. It keeps competing interests at bay. It's like – hmmm...

(pause)

Nobleman: It keeps things working smoothly for everybody.

Wendy: Does that in turn serve the people, or is the city more serving itself?

Nobleman: Not really serving the people so much. It's not a democratic thing, you know. This isn't a democracy. It's more like serving, accommodating or directing those that make things happen.

Wendy: Who makes things happen?

Nobleman: The nobility, the merchants, the military – anybody who makes things happen, goes through me. I don't necessarily give orders as they have to go through me to iron things out.

Wendy: So I'm hearing you're the facilitator. You make things happen.

Nobleman: I'm the one who removes the hiccoughs.

Wendy: *(laughing)* What a great description.

Nobleman: So the stuff happens without...hmmm, how to explain this...

(pause)

Wendy: You remove obstacles?

Nobleman: Yes, so there isn't conflict, so things can move forward.

Wendy: Okay. Tell me more.

Simon: *(happily)* I'm the edge-smoother!

Wendy: *(smiling)* Excellent. What a perfect description.

(pause as she formulates her next question)

Wendy: What was your life purpose – does it feel like you're on track?

Nobleman: This feels very much like my life as the plantation manager, as *(name deleted)* hmmm – whatever his name was. You know who I mean.

Wendy: Yes, your most recent past life you found in a previous session? You see a parallel there?

Nobleman: Yes, very much. His job was to be the interface between the plantation owner and the workers – to make it smooth, so there wasn't conflict.

Wendy: Yes?

Nobleman: In this case it's the same thing, to be a smoother-over, to make things work. There's a lot of power, but I don't need to use a lot of power as it's well understood that things need to go through me.

(pause)

Nobleman: It's not a matter of commanding people that you have to do this or that.

Wendy: So you're wielding your power very lightly? You're more influencing?

Nobleman: More making it clear nothing is going to happen, nobody is going to benefit without creating an agreement, without my smoothing the edges, without my melding all the concerns. That's my job, to make sure everybody benefits.

Wendy: So you're –

Nobleman: *(interrupting excitedly)* I'm the Lord High Mayor!

(Note: She googled "Lord High Mayor" after their session as neither was familiar with the title – fits for the time and place. Excellent confirmation of Simon's memory.)

Wendy: Wonderful! You're the Lord High Mayor. Are you saying people want to continue these arrangements because there's something in it for everyone?

Lord High Mayor: Yes. It's like I'm holding the prosperity of the town and the interests of everybody in my hands. I am the Smoother-Over.

Wendy: Very good. So it's a purpose-driven life.

Lord High Mayor: Yes!

(pause)

Wendy: Did you have a family in that lifetime?

(no reply)

Wendy: Do you have a sense of your parents, any siblings, possibly a wife or children?

Lord High Mayor: No immediate sense of that comes to mind, though it's less independent than that other life we just viewed. It was completely independent.

(pause)

Lord High Mayor: Now I have an inkling of having a wife, for example.

(pause)

Lord High Mayor: It's like a functionary wife, not a real wife that I was interested in, for example. It's very nebulous; it's more like a dutiful thing...

Wendy: Was it expected for someone in your position to have a wife, to marry in that time and place?

Lord High Mayor: Yes. It's not a love-match.

Wendy: Understand. There are many reasons for marriage. They can be arranged or necessary. Desired or not.

(pause)

Wendy: Is your wife from that life in your life now?

Lord High Mayor: No, this person is very grey. Not important. It doesn't bring anybody to mind.

Wendy: So like a place-holder?

Lord High Mayor: That's one way to describe it, yes.

Wendy: Is there anyone from that lifetime in your life now?

Lord High Mayor: Hmmm. No, nobody comes to mind from either relationship clues or physiology clues – there's nothing jumping out at me.

Wendy: Trust your instinct. You would know their energy, regardless of appearance. You're very aware of the soul essence.

(Pause as she considers if it's time to wrap this portion up and segue.)

Wendy: Is there anything more you can learn from that time and that place?

Lord High Mayor: I learned I could be highly effective without having to wield power.

Wendy: Wonderful, that's a profound lesson. Is that attractive to you?

Lord High Mayor: Oh, yeah, it beats the alternative!

Wendy: The alternative of being either ineffective, or having to use a lot of force?

(She was subtly providing Simon an opportunity to answer his own question whether he had a lot of Viking or Viking type lives as he suspected. If so, why? Was there anything for him to release or learn in that area?)

Lord High Mayor: Both. Any time power is created by threat, you give away that power. Power hinted at or power by reputation is much better. A more effective mover.

Wendy: Excellent! Is there anything more to explore or learn from that time and place?

(long pause)

Lord High Mayor: Collaboration was fun and easy, and invigorating.

Wendy: Wonderful – so collaboration made it fun and easy.

Lord High Mayor: Yes. It just made everything flow. It made everything worth pursuing. It made everything worthwhile.

Wendy: Fantastic! You've explored this quite thoroughly.

(She moved Simon to the next scene. He was at a much deeper level of trance during his next life visioning. No more long pauses in his speech, and his body was much more relaxed and still.)

III: THE WORLD WAR II SOLDIER

Wendy: You've now moved to an important scene to bring you healing or information today. What's the first thing you see?

Simon: *(chuckling happily as new past life persona)* Hmmm... There's landing craft. Look at them!

(Wendy thought quickly, uncertain if Simon is talking about military landing craft, and if so, Earth-based or ET. Simon had ET questions on his list for the session. There was a possibility some had been harming his kidneys. She unconsciously narrowed her eyes and leaned forward on high alert due to the combination of his question and his description of where he had landed.)

Wendy: *(speaking quickly and a bit sternly)* What type of landing craft? What do they look like, and what are they used for?

Simon: The World War II type used for invading beaches.

25

Wendy: *(relaxing)* Got it. Great job – very specific. Carry on your natural course. What are you doing? What's happening now?

(Sensing he might be seasick, as she had been with him at sea in several lifetimes and suddenly felt quite nauseous.)

Simon: It's just us, slapping up and down hard on the waves. There's a bunch of us aboard. Some of us are sick.

Wendy: Where are you landing?

(pause)

Simon: *(matter-of-factly)* Don't know yet. You can't know ahead.

Wendy: How does your body feel?

Simon: I'm one of the ones that are sick. Upchucking and very, very nervous.

Wendy: Are you young, or old, or middle-aged?

Simon: Young.

Wendy: What is your exact age?

Simon: Nineteen.

Wendy: You're nineteen. What's your name?

Simon: Robert.

Wendy: Robert. Hello, Robert. Where are you from?

(pause)

Simon *(speaking as Robert)*: Ohio.

Wendy: Ohio. You're from Ohio. What's happening now?

(no reply)

Wendy: *(Struggling with the military terminology.)* You can see your ship – your boat –

your – uhhh – landing craft – uhhh – land on the beach...

(no reply)

Wendy: What happens next?

Robert: Not much. There's not much resistance. We get into tanks, and go along the coastal road.

Wendy: Were the tanks waiting for you and you were able to get safely aboard those?

Robert: No, the tanks came ashore.

Wendy: Where did the tanks come from?

(Doesn't understand yet the tanks were aboard the landing craft with Robert.)

Robert: The tanks came aboard I think at Sicily.

Wendy: Okay. Very good. You're doing great. What else do you see?

Robert: It looks like Sicily.

Wendy: Great, Sicily. So you're in Italy. You can clearly see your tank. How many men are in your tank?

Robert: Well, there's a tank crew. I'm not part of the tank crew. There's a bunch of us riding up on the tank, along these coastal roads.

Wendy: Describe it –

(Robert interrupts – a great sign – visualizing very clearly – vibration in room going up as his trance level deepens.)

Robert: So there's, I don't know, 5 to 8 of us riding on the tank. Sitting on the tank itself was kind of uncomfortable. We try and sit on coils of rope or equipment bags, something on the tank itself to be more comfortable.

Wendy: Are there multiple tanks driving along together, or do you go separately?

Robert: It's a long column of tanks.

Wendy: Okay. What else do you see as you ride along on the tank?

Robert: We're up above the water. The coast is on the left. We're following a road, heading into a town.

Wendy: Just continue on your natural course. Do you get to the town?

Robert: We get to the town. It seems to be pretty well shot up. Not a lot of people lurking about. They retreated somewhere.

Wendy: So what happens next? Do you move through the town, or does anything occur in the town?

Robert: We move on through the town. Moving, always moving. Very little stoppage time.

Wendy: Okay. What happens next? Is the scenery much the same, or do you see some changes?

Robert: The only thing that changes is the towns. We move through multiple towns.

Wendy: So you're going through town after town. Do they look primarily the same? Do you see signs of confrontation and battle in many towns? Do you see many people, or are most people gone or hiding?

Robert: In some of the towns people come out. We're not in the front wave of the fighting, so we're not seeing a lot of shots. We're not getting artillery barrages.

Wendy: What concerns you the most for your safety?

Robert: We have to be most concerned about enemy planes.

Wendy: So there's a little land resistance, but not much. You're more concerned about the planes – enemy planes?

Robert: Yeah, because we're a long line of tanks.

Wendy: So you're very visible.

Robert: *(laconically)* Yeah, you got it. The planes won't get whoever is IN the tanks, but whoever is ON the tanks is gonna get splattered if they're not careful.

(Note: Speech feels authentic for a young man in that time and place – not Simon's typical well-educated vocabulary or speech.)

Wendy: I understand. How do you watch for the planes? Is someone on lookout, or is literally everyone watching?

Robert: *(nodding hard)* Yeah, everyone is watching – everyone. You got it.

Wendy: What would you do if you spot a plane or planes – would you be able to fit inside the tank, would you stop and take cover, would you fire back – what do you do?

Robert: Some are firing back, but it's useless. The planes are too far away. So you hop off, and you get in between the tanks while they keep moving. You get in front of one tank, and behind another.

Wendy: So you take cover between the tanks, front to back? They move slowly enough you can just walk along, or do you have to jog or run at times?

Robert: Slow and easy, but always on the move. Yeah, front to back and into the sides of the tanks, too.

(pause)

Robert: Coverts. Like coverts do.

Wendy: Oh?

(Stalling for time as she formulates her next question. Has no idea what coverts do. Were coverts on a secret mission, implying a covert operation? Getting ready to ask, when Robert changes the subject.)

Robert: And rocks.

Wendy: *(puzzled)* Rocks?

Robert: Sometimes you could take cover behind rocks.

Wendy: Oh, I see. Do you have to do that many times?

Robert: Not too many times. There's a lot of false alarms because there's U.S. planes up there, too. Allied forces, ya know...

Wendy: Yes.

Robert: Everybody is pretty nervous, because you can't tell which side until they're really close.

Wendy: Yes. So it's hard to tell, friend or foe. Hence the many false alarms. But friendly fire is just as deadly as enemy fire, isn't it?

Robert: Yeah.

Wendy: It must be nerve-wracking. How are you feeling, Robert? You're a young man, how are you coping with being on enemy grounds? Is this your first time away from home?

Robert: I think I was in North Africa before this. I wasn't completely new, but I was still nervous. I still haven't seen a lot of combat. I'm not a seasoned veteran yet.

Wendy: What happens next?

Robert: Hmmm...

(She senses a major energy change in room, so grounds herself once more and prepares for something important.)

Robert: OHHHH!

Wendy: *(calmly)* What's happening?

Robert: Flashbacks.

Wendy: Where are you flashing back to?

Robert: Ireland. I think I'm....I think I'm Irish. I think I'm having flashbacks.

Wendy: What are you feeling, Robert, as you experience these flashbacks to Ireland?

(Testing his name to see if he had leapfrogged to another life, as suddenly talking about Ireland vs. Italy or the U.S.? Why?)

Wendy: You don't need to feel any discomfort, you're completely safe now.

Robert: I don't see the battle, but I'm already down. It feels like a gut wound.

Wendy: *(firmly)* Know that you don't need to feel any discomfort now as you go through these battlefield moments as Robert. You're poised to learn something important here – you can do this!

(She sends Reiki healing energy to him from her chair when she sees him unconsciously place both hands over his mid-section. She had the sense he

31

---

was trying to keep his organs inside his body, and wondered if this correlated to the digestive issues he now experienced from time-to-time. She made a note to ask for healing in this area when they went to the Healing Temple.)

Robert: I keep flashing back to Ireland.

(Pause as she tries to recall the geography and her World War II history. Was Ireland in World War II? She didn't think so, but couldn't google real-time from her phone as was using it to record.)

Wendy: Did you travel to Ireland after Sicily?

Robert: No, I'm still in Italy, but as I lie there I think of Ireland. I think I'm from Ireland originally that lifetime. I was born there, or my ancestry is there...

Wendy: Oh, I see. So you've been wounded in that tank column as Robert, and you're lying there in Sicily, flashing back to your early life in Ireland, before you lived in Ohio and possibly traveled to N. Africa?

Robert: *(sounding pleased)* Exactly! You got it. But I don't know I was wounded in the tank column. It was either that or we may have been walking through town or in a field.

(pause)

Robert: It doesn't matter. There was a sense of us always pushing, always moving.

(Long pause during which he began exhibiting a lot of restlessness.)

Wendy: *(soothingly)* What's happening now, Robert? This was a long time ago. You're just fine now.

(Sending him Reiki life force healing again.)

Robert: I'm lying on the ground – there's such a cold feeling. The cold - the cold in the belly. Then these quick flashbacks – these vignettes.

Wendy: Are you alone, or is anyone around you?

Robert: They're with me. They're trying to keep me warm.

(He unconsciously pulls up his own blanket, the same one he'd argued with her about at the start of his session and told her he wouldn't need.)

Wendy: *(gently)* Are they giving you medical attention?

Robert: Yes.

Wendy: *(soothingly)* It's okay. You're okay. Are you outdoors or indoors?

Robert: I'm outdoors.

Wendy: Are the Medics or your friends putting a blanket over you, or jackets or something else?

Robert: Blanket.

Wendy: *(calmly, anticipating he's dropping his body and crossing back over to Home)* We can see and feel that blanket bringing you great comfort and warmth. You can pull it up higher if you like. You're just fine. What happens next?

Robert: *(more calmly)* There's lots of rapid-order flashbacks. Then they just stop.

Wendy: Let's move to the end of that particular life, where you've passed over into the hereafter. This will be easy for you – you've done it many times before. I can help you if necessary.

(She does need to help him cross over to the Light.)

Wendy: Now that you look back on that lifetime and see what you had to learn from it, what do you think was the reason for visiting that lifetime?

Robert: Hmmm. I would say building camaraderie. I have a lot of solitary lives, it seems like. This one didn't feel solitary. I had my chums, so to speak.

Wendy: Because you had comrades, you had friends, you had "the unit?"

Robert: *(sounding pleased)* Exactly! I had friends, I had guys from high school with me, for instance.

(pause)

Wendy: What else built the feeling of camaraderie?

(long pause)

Robert: Oh, I see. We had gone to boot camp together, to training, some of us stayed in the same unit. We went into combat and we felt lucky we didn't have a lot of real resistance at first. So you felt fortunate for that.

Wendy: *(nodding)* Yes. Is there anyone there to greet you as you move into the Light at the end of that lifetime as Robert? We'd like to learn more what that lifetime was about. I'm requesting a Greeter for you.

IV: SPIRIT GUIDE REUNION

(Simon immediately begins laughing harder and harder. Vibration in room goes much higher. Finally, he is able to speak.)

Simon: *(gleefully)* You miserable fuck!

(Wendy was startled by his unusual reaction to crossing over, and trying very hard not to laugh, too. She knew he wasn't directing his remark to her – she sensed a huge Guide.)

Wendy: Who is your Greeter?

Simon: It's *(Guide name deleted)*! It's the same old shit. Some sort of comic act!

Wendy: What is he doing?

Simon: He's R.F.'ing me. *(bragging and being nonchalant at the same time)* He's playing peek-a-boo with me. He always does that in some sort of fashion. He does this every time!

(pause)

Simon: *(laughing)* Now I'm in this form, now I'm not! Guess who I am? He fucks with me every time!

(Wendy finally bursts into laughter, too, as Simon was so delighted to be Home. She was so thrilled he was finally connecting so strongly with one of his Guides.)

Wendy: *(smiling widely)* Enjoy your reunion. He has a message for you as to how well you did this lifetime. You can sense what he's thinking. Ask him – ask them, as you may find other Guides or Beings of Light there, too – how well you did in that life. He will answer you.

(pause)

(Vibration level falls abruptly in room. Simon sounds very left-brained and analytical when he replies.)

Simon: How's he going to answer me?

Wendy: He's going to tell you how well you did in your life as Robert. Ask him how well you did that lifetime, please.

Simon: *(still sounding puzzled)* Out loud, or just ask him?

Wendy: You can ask him via telepathy, or aloud.

Simon: *(lecturing her a bit)* Well, it takes place there via telepathy. You know that. We've talked about this so many times...

Wendy: *(firmly)* Yes. So use your excellent telepathy skills we both know you have, and tell me what he says for your recording.

(pause)

Simon: How? Remind me how we did the telepathy before. We were good! You and I still use telepathy with each other now in our current lives, don't we?

(Wendy considered the implications briefly to make sure he would not be confused as to time and place before recapping their first lives together. She reminded him they had chosen a series of three silent monastery lives in a row. They had quickly perfected their telepathy on Earth as they weren't allowed to speak to each other in the monasteries where they had scribed, yet had so much to say to each other.

She knew this was an unusual gift to remember their telepathy skills so profoundly while incarnated on Earth. It had been wonderful when they were dating, and then very hard on her once they had broken up as she didn't want to feel their connection continue so strongly.)

Simon: *(nodding)* Oh, okay. Got it. I remember now. He's like *(referring to his Guide)* "No sweat! You did what you needed to do. You got what you needed to get."

Wendy: Very good. What else?

Simon: It wasn't an extraordinary lifetime. A nineteen-year-old. But it was to experience that camaraderie, to move out of those solitary lives...

Wendy: Excellent. A transition, perhaps?

(no reply)

Wendy: How do you feel about his words, his communication to you?

(pause)

Simon: Well, I certainly don't doubt him.

(pause)

Simon: It's reassuring. You never want to think that you failed.

Wendy: Did you complete your main mission?

Simon: I don't know that – it doesn't feel like there really was one.

Wendy: Wasn't it to experience camaraderie? I just heard you say that was part of your life mission. To move out of the solitary lives.

Simon: It was just to experience...*(trailing off)*

(long pause)

Wendy: It's *all* just experiences. Isn't that why we come to Earth School, to progress via experiences? You've expressed that belief to me many times.

Simon: It was just to experience – ahhh – togetherness, esprit de corps, camaraderie.

Wendy: Yes.

Simon: Being a part of something, when that wasn't my usual M.O. *(modus operandi)*

Wendy: Was there anything you could have done better in that lifetime? What does he say specifically to you as he gives you your life review? You can hear him NOW.

(Simon bursts into long, uproarious laughter again. Vibration in room immediately goes much higher.)

Simon: Oh, fuck!

(She laughs in surprise, too, as Simon continues to literally snort with laughter. She needed to suggest he take a bathroom break soon.)

Wendy: What's he saying to you? You're hearing your Guide really clearly now.

(Simon slaps his thighs in uproarious laughter.)

Simon: He says, "Robert, you could have been a better shot!"

Wendy: *(laughing)* And there's the humor of the other side! Just enjoy it, which you clearly are.

Simon: *(laughing heartily)* Oh, you miserable little fuck.

(pause)

Simon: He just keeps taunting me, "You could have been a better shot."

(He continues to laugh boisterously.)

Simon: Oh, God. He says, "You might still be alive now, if you were just a better shot!"

Wendy: Humor from the other side of the Veil can express like this because we're eternal souls – there's not really such a thing as "death," as you know – we just drop our bodies or our life forms from time-to-time.

Simon: *(settling down)* Exactly.

Wendy: What does he look like? What is he wearing, and is this his normal presentation? You know *(Guide name deleted)* very well, and he certainly knows and loves you completely.

Simon: He's just over-the-top. He's done this since the first time I met him. He's got on this jester outfit. He's got his hands like this...

(demonstrating)

(pause)

Wendy: Why? It feels like there's a reason...

Simon: *(settling down more)* Ohhhh – I see now. He knows how to make me not take myself too seriously.

Wendy: *(nodding)* That's very healing, isn't it?

(long pause)

(Palpable energy change in room – vibration increases – Simon moves into a deeper level of trance – begins to speak as his Higher Self or possibly as the Light? Voice and energy much more serene, with a sense of deep wisdom.)

Simon's Higher Self: Yes. Kind of like you've learned to do. More lightness of being. Your energy is so different now than when we first re-met a few years ago. You've released a lot.

Wendy: *(feeling deeply touched and grateful)* Thank you. How do you feel in that place? Do you feel the peace and the unconditional love?

Simon: Well, his way is to gird me for that. That's his way of decompression. So he starts trifling with me right away, and I can relate immediately, as that's so much of my family M.O.

Wendy: Yes, because in your family a good insult means "I love you."

Simon: Exactly! You get it. You and I used to have fun being snarky with each other. A lot of people don't understand loving sarcasm, but you do, and we're both quick-witted. We were an even match, or I wouldn't have been sarcastic with you.

(pause)

Wendy: *(smiling)* Agreed. Our verbal jousting was a lot of fun.

Simon: In my family we insult each other. *(Guide name deleted)* does that too, to take your mind off the stuff, whether it's dying or ummm – worries about performance, or ahhh – the serious questions like did I meet my match, did I fulfill my mission?

(pause)

Simon: He just gets it out of that. It's a good transition for me.

Wendy: *(nodding)* Absolutely.

Simon: *(snorting)* "You might be alive if you were a better shot!"

Wendy: *(laughing heartily)* That is our quote of the day!

Simon: It's like I can't get EVEN with him and I SO want to get even with him. He knows that, and he just grins!

(pause)

Simon: "Buck up – there's nothing you can do," is what he's telling me.

Wendy: What's the best way for you to sense more easily *(Guide's name deleted)* presence in your daily life, as well as that of your other Guides? How can you have this amazing connection and guidance every day like you do right at this moment? This would be so beneficial for you.

(long pause)

Simon: Oh. I get it now. You're right.

(long pause as he considers her question)

Simon: Well, ask more, I guess.

Wendy: Yes. And what else?

Simon: Well, just like when you're in the Green Room in a Life-Between-Lives before you're born, you work out your signals.

Wendy: During the pre-life planning segment?

Simon: No, later. When you're in the Ready Room, when you're ready to launch into a new life, you work the review of your signals so you know when you're meeting someone significant. We ought to work out signals.

Wendy: For you to know when your Guides are near?

Simon: When he's trying to get a hold of me, and when I'm trying to reach him.

Wendy: Okay.

Simon: And not just him, all of them.

Wendy: Exactly. Your entire team. You have a large team of Guides as I've sensed several of them, most especially your *(Ancestor name deleted)* and your *(Ancestor name deleted)*, and you're aware of additional Guides.

(no reply)

Wendy: So what's the most effective way for you to easily connect with each of your Guides? Do you need to be funny about it and literally pick up your cell phone and pretend to call him? You know – "Can you hear me, can you hear me now?" The old cell phone commercials?

Simon: *(smiling)* Yes, that would work with him. If I get funny with him, it will get back at him, and we'll connect. *(Guide name deleted)* tends to be more serious, *(Guide name deleted)* is very spiritual, very considerate, and *(Guide name deleted)* is...

(pause)

Simon: They're each different, you know?

Wendy: Yes. You have a well-rounded team ready to help you at any time. We all do. So let's get this energetic pathway built straight to you. A super-highway of your Guides coming directly to you!

Simon: *(nodding)* With him, something humorous.

Wendy: So is it as simple as you asking them to come closer, and to feel and see and hear their presence more easily?

Simon: No, that's the beginning. But it always seems things are heightened when there is a code word or a secret signal or a secret handshake or a symbol that you use to visualize, so if you visualize it, BOOM!, they're there for you!

Wendy: You planned that before you came to Earth for this life. What is your secret signal with each of your Guides? It can be different with each one.

(pause)

Simon: *(sounding surprised)* I don't know that I did plan that.

Wendy: Well, we can create it now. This explains why it's been so hard for you to connect with them. Each Being of Light has a unique energy signature. You clearly know them well, and they know and love and support you on every level. How can you establish easier direct pathways between you and each of your Guides?

(long pause)

Simon: They're saying "Just set the table."

Wendy: So you're just to set the table, and ask them to join you? Is it that simple?

(long pause)

Wendy: Is there anything more your Guides will tell you about how to easily connect with them?

Simon: *(holds his right hand up in a stop signal)* Hold on. Don't talk. I'm setting the table. I'm doing the work with them right now. Almost got it.

(long pause)

Simon: *(huge smile)* Okay. Got it!

Wendy: *(beaming)* Wonderful! So now it's done. This is fantastic! I'm so happy for you.

(They had been working on his connection with his Guides for several years because his Guides began coming to her when Simon couldn't yet perceive them. This was a huge breakthrough! Wendy guided Simon they would now move to a Place of All Knowledge to get the answers to his questions he had written before they began that morning.)

V: THE PLACE OF ALL KNOWLEDGE

Wendy: This is a tremendous breakthrough with your Guides. I am so thrilled for you! Really solid work. Look around you – can you see the Light?

Simon: *(hesitating)* Clarify.

Wendy: You're at Home now - you've crossed over. You were just with your Guides in a profound way. You are now at the Place of All Knowledge. Can you see the White Light of Home?

Simon: I don't know. I see a landscape with a lot of different lights.

Wendy: Okay, super, let's explore it. What *do* you see? Focus there.

Simon: It's like a moonscape, with lots of shadows – beams of light. Billowing vents of light like from volcanic spew, but with light instead of smoke.

Wendy: Okay. Does it feel –

Simon: *(interrupting excitedly)* Aurora borealis lights!

Wendy: Oh, the Northern Lights, how beautiful! Does it feel completely loving and peaceful to you?

Simon: Yes, of course.

Wendy: Wonderful. You can now slowly move more into that Light, and through that Light if you wish. You can merge with it.

(She helps Simon merge with the Light to raise his vibration and comprehension.)

(long pause)

Wendy: What are you seeing or experiencing now?

Simon: I see people in balconies. Tiers and tiers of balconies, situated kind of like being at the Opera.

Wendy: Very good.

Simon: Bunches and bunches and bunches of them.

Wendy: In this place, do you feel there is a source of Supreme Intelligence all around?

Simon: I don't get that specifically, no.

Wendy: Okay. How do you feel about seeing all of those people up in those multiple balconies? Are they observing you?

Simon: No, I don't get that sense. They're just there.

Wendy: Okay. What else do you notice?

Simon: They're just going about their business, as am I. I'm not on a stage, or being presented for review.

Wendy: Would you like to remain there longer, or to move to a Temple of Healing?

Simon: I want to stay here.

Wendy: Of course. Stay there as long as you want, and just feel the bliss and the wonderful experience of being Home. I'm going to excuse myself to use the bathroom. I'll be just outside your room and can hear you. When I return, you can tell me when you're ready to move on.

(pause – she returns)

Simon: I need to go to the loo, too. My God, we needed that laugh!

(pause)

Wendy: *(smiling)* Yes, we did. You're doing great work, *(name deleted)*. You can sit up slowly on the edge of your bed now – walk carefully to the bathroom. When you return, we'll resume right where we are now. It will be easy for you to reconnect even deeper than before.

(He returns a moment later.)

Simon: You need to help me go back into that energy – go backwards a bit.

Wendy: *(nodding)* Yes, of course. Where would you like to go back to?

Simon: Back to where I was merging in with the Light.

(pause)

Wendy: Certainly. Know that you are one with the Light...

(Repeats process for Simon to merge with the Light.)

VI: A PLACE OF HEALING

Wendy: As things become clear, I would like you to tell me what you see around you. What do you see?

Simon: Some mist, and waterfalls, some wheels –

*(Wendy sees a possible dungeon and some equipment she doesn't like – were those large wheels to turn on a wooden torture device? This felt so energetically **wrong**, especially in a Place of Healing.)*

Wendy: *(sharply)* Wheels? What kind of wheels. Describe them now!

Simon: Oh, I see, they're Ferris wheels – I see light beams snaking around corners.

Wendy: *(relaxing as the dungeons faded away)* Wonderful. What else?

Simon: Lots of leaves – things are half-hidden – going around corners, hidden, I'm not on a straight path. You have to follow them as they curve around, to see what's there. Lots of landscapes...

(pause)

Wendy: You may feel the Source of healing is even stronger in this place. How do you feel in this place of healing?

Simon: *(excitedly)* Like I'm being compelled by a magnet – like I'm being pulled forward! I know right where to go.

Wendy: Wonderful! You're doing great. Now you will see a light. The light will go to a particular part of your body to heal it. Which part of your body does the light go to first?

Simon: *(sounding surprised)* My feet! My left foot first.

Wendy: *(biting her tongue – no bad jokes allowed)* What color is this first light that goes to your left foot, to your feet?

Simon: It's kind of white and pinkish.

Wendy: You can feel this light energy doing its healing work now. What does it feel like?

Simon. I don't really *feel* it – it has a *look* to it, not a feel.

Wendy: Okay. Know that the light is healing your feet. We're just going to let it do its work for a minute. We will leave that pinkish-white light there to heal your feet.

(pause)

Wendy: A new light should appear – where does it go?

Simon: It goes to my back.

Wendy: Fantastic. What color is the new light that goes to your back?

Simon: A very light blue.

Wendy: You can feel that light blue energy doing its work. What does it feel like as it completely heals your back?

Simon: *(frowning)* Again, it doesn't really have a feeling. It has a look.

Wendy: Okay, enjoy the look of that light as it heals your entire back, making it perfect. Enjoy the look of it as it continues its work. We're going to let it do its powerful healing.

(no reply)

Wendy: *(upbeat)* We will leave that light blue light with your back until it is completely healed. You deserve this healing, and it's going to happen today!

(pause)

Wendy: A new light should appear. Where does it go on your body?

Simon: My head and neck.

Wendy: Ok, we're healing your head and neck. What does the light look or feel like as it radiates to heal your head and neck?

Simon: It feels like pulling cords.

(She focused even more sharply as some would consider this psychic surgery.)

Wendy: Excellent. This will be very safe and gentle for you, and also completely effective.

(pause)

Wendy: What does this latest light look like?

Simon: It's kind of a purplish chrysanthemum color.

(pause)

Wendy: *(continuing to work to get him to be able to feel)* What does it feel like?

Simon: It's like strings of yarn are being pulled from me.

Wendy: Wonderful! Let those strings be safely and effectively fully removed from your head and neck. Enjoy the feeling of your healing as it restores your head and neck to perfect health. We're going to give it a moment to do that.

(pause)

Wendy: We will leave that chrysanthemum purplish color there to fully heal your neck and head. A new light should appear – where does it go to heal you?

(no reply)

Wendy: Where does the new light go?

Simon: It goes to my knee.

Wendy: What color is the new light that goes to your knee?

Simon: It's black.

(Wendy masks her surprise, as color unusual. Chooses to follow client's lead as he was very peaceful, and working extremely well with the healing lights. In hindsight, she could have asked him if black was the highest vibration color to heal his knee.)

Wendy: It's black. What does the energy radiating from that black color feel like, or are you seeing it or sensing it?

Simon: I don't feel it at all – I see it.

Wendy: Okay. Well enjoy seeing that black healing light and know it is radiating to heal your knees. Let that black light, that strong healing energy continue to heal you.

(pause)

Simon: *(nodding)* I am.

Wendy: A new light should appear – where does it go?

Simon: My torso – my stomach.

Wendy: Wonderful. What color is the new light that goes to your stomach and torso?

Simon: White.

Wendy: It's white. Let that white light heal your stomach and torso very gently and effectively. We'll let it continue its beautiful, complete healing for your digestive system, from your death as Robert in World War II, and for anything else needed.

(pauses to allow time for the healing)

Wendy: A new colored light should now appear – where does it go?

Simon: Heart. It goes to my heart.

Wendy: What color is the new light that goes to your heart?

Simon: Green.

Wendy: Wonderful! Enjoy seeing that green color as it completely fills your heart and radiates to heal you. Feel your heart open to be very loving and giving and peaceful. We'll allow that green light to stay there and heal you heart while a new light appears, and goes to a different location on your body. Where does the new light go?

Simon: My lower back.

Wendy: What color is the new light that goes to your lower back?

Simon: It's crème-colored, like a fudgsicle.

Wendy: *(smiling at his description)* Well, enjoy seeing that crème-colored light as it completely heals your lower back right now. Let it just radiate and make your lower back perfect again. Know it will continue to do its work as long as necessary.

(pauses to allow time for the healing)

Wendy: A new light should appear and come to you – where does it go?

(pause)

Simon: *(animated tone)* I get a rainbow of colors, and they're going all around me – they don't go any particular place, they just keep swirling all around me!

Wendy: Wonderful! Enjoy that beautiful healing rainbow, and let the lights go all around you where they need to go. See and feel all those colors very clearly, let them encircle your entire four-body system, your aura, your etheric body. See them going wherever they need to go to heal you completely.

(Allows time for him to experience all the healing lights.)

Wendy: Is there a new light to heal you, or are the lights complete with the rainbow?

(pause)

Simon: No new light.

Wendy: You're doing such strong work. Know that you will clearly see and feel these exact same energies as you listen back to your MP3. Remain here for a moment longer, and really imprint that healing energy. Know that you can return to this experience at any time, including when you fall asleep at night. You'll then receive healing all night long and no longer wake up feeling worked over. Do you feel confident you can do that, or do you need more instruction?

(Thinking ahead to ensure he can heal any new injuries on his own, particularly as he is still a competitive athlete in a contact sport.)

(no reply)

Wendy: Does that feel complete for you?

(Sensing another color? Energy shift in room – Simon at a lighter trance level.)

Simon: *(sounding very left-brained again)* Complete for what? The colors?

Wendy: Yes, the colors are the healing lights for you. Did you say the rainbow felt like the last one, or is there more?

Simon: There's an orange one coming through now – I don't know where it wants to go.

Wendy: That's okay – you're doing great – just let that orange light come, and go wherever it needs to go – your heart, your body, your mind, your soul. Just let that orange color come in. Visualize the color orange clearly and strongly now – see it, smell it, taste it. You're doing great!

(pause)

Wendy: Are there any new lights that need to come to you?

Simon: None that seem to be trying right now.

Wendy: Okay, know that they can come in whenever they need to. You now know how to do this work extremely well. You're a master visualizer for healing now, just like you are for athletics – you have to *see* it first to be able to *feel* it, then to *do* it, and finally to *be* it at the highest level. They're stages. Do you understand?

Simon: *(nodding)* Yes.

Wendy: Wonderful. Then let's move on.

VII: MERGING WITH THE HIGHER SELF

Wendy: You may now visit a Place or Temple of Knowledge, if you wish.

Simon: What's there?

Wendy: This is where you go to work out your lifetimes before you come to Earth. You can get answers to any and all of your questions.

(no reply)

Wendy: Is it appropriate you visit such a place in order to learn something new?

Simon: *(wryly)* I don't know if it's appropriate, never my long suit, but it seems to be useful.

Wendy: *(laughing)* Wonderful. We will now go to a Place of Knowledge. As you enter and see what's around you, you can tell me what you see around you. What does it look like?

(no reply)

Wendy: What does the Place of Knowledge look like?

(no reply)

Wendy: There's normally somewhere there to help you navigate this place. Who do you see – what do they look like? You're going to get something NOW!

(long pause – vibration rises in room)

(Simon's voice and energy changes as he enters a deeper level of trance.)

Simon *(or Simon's Higher Self)*: The place is very layered. It has lots of carvings, lots of symbols. Lots of motifs.

(pause)

Simon: I'm just getting a look around. There's no one particularly to greet me.

Wendy: Okay.

Simon: There's one guy I can see. He looks a little odd – like he's got a cardinal's hat on – like from a Catholic Church?

Wendy: Yes?

Simon: It's one of those skull cap things.

Wendy: Great. You're doing very well. Just continue exploring.

Simon: He's definitely an odd duck.

Wendy: *(smiling)* Do you interact, or are you each just doing your own thing?

Simon: No interaction.

Wendy: Okay. You're observing him. We would appreciate someone coming forward to help you navigate this place, and to answer the important questions you brought with you today. Is there someone who can come forward and speak with you?

(Long pause – vibration in room goes much higher.)

Simon*: (sounding awed)* Ohhhh! I'm not sure, but I think it's my Higher Self!

Wendy: Fantastic! Be very confident, if you sense your Higher Self, that is who is coming forward for you. You can now merge more fully with your Higher Self. This is wonderful – great work!

(She paused to allow him time to connect.)

Wendy: Is your Higher Self happy to see you?

(Simon begins to speak as his Higher Self.)

Simon's Higher Self: It's – he's ? – not expressing that. He's trying to give more iconic views of who I am, who he is – who it is.

Wendy: Please share that iconic info with me aloud when the views first come to you so you have them for your recording. It will help you recall this clearly to continue to connect deeply with your Higher Self on a daily basis. This is marvelous work!

(pause)

Wendy: Your Higher Self has all the knowledge, everything you need to know about yourself across all space and time. We are able to ask your Higher Self your important questions, and he will be able to give you any appropriate answer for your highest good. Know that he is telepathically linked to you and can hear my words through you.

(pause)

Wendy: I'm now going to ask your Higher Self your questions. Is your *(title deleted)* in your primary soul group – why does he not appear to be there?

(Long pause – vibration falls.)

Simon: We may have to come back to that. There's nothing coming up.

(He sounds disappointed, having asked this question before in other sessions and not having received any clarity. She realizes she should have started with a softball question, knowing his frustration in this area.)

Wendy: That's fine. We'll return to that question.

Simon: Symbolically, it's like curtains shutting.

Wendy: You're seeing the images so clearly now – please tell me what you see immediately, like when you sensed the curtains closing. We only wish to be shown what's for your highest good today. More clarity will come when you listen to your recording, or when you read it, if you transcribe your session.

(pause)

Wendy: Let's proceed to your next question for your Higher Self and the Light.

(Pause as she scans his list.)

Wendy: Do you meet a soul partner only every second or third lifetime? What can the Higher Self tell us about that?

(long pause)

Higher Self: It's not a clear sounding gong, but it seems to be a very distinctive *yes*, because it's so all-consuming. You couldn't go through every lifetime like that. It's – so – so – all–consuming.

Wendy: What's all-consuming, the sound of the gong, or...?

Higher Self: No, the nature of – of – uhhh – it...

(long pause)

Wendy: The nature of being in a romance with a soul mate or life partner?

Simon: *(trance level dropping - struggling for words)* Like that. What you said. It's just – I don't know how you even work, or have any other – ummm – other things that you do...

Wendy: So it's –

Simon: *(interrupting)* You'd have to be rich and have no other duties.

(Wendy's eyebrows shot up. She worked to mask her surprise and tone carefully, knowing everyone has their own reality. It was critical she respect his, without judgment, yet clarify what he needed to understand this area more fully.)

Wendy: *(in a careful neutral tone)* Are you saying you feel you'd have to be rich and have no other duties to have a successful romantic relationship?

(Vibration in room rises as Higher Self comes in.)

Higher Self: *(bluntly, without hesitation)* Yes. True for him right now.

Wendy: Am I hearing what's right for you at this time in your soul development is to meet a soul mate every second or third lifetime? Is that right – does that answer your question?

Higher Self: Yes. It seems to.

Wendy: Excellent.

Higher Self: But more so, it seems to explain the *why* to something he already knew.

Wendy: So when you are in a relationship with a soul mate or life partner – who can be one of several people – you don't make other progress? Is that what the Higher Self wants us to know?

Simon: *(exhibiting some frustration – the Higher Self doesn't feel frustration)* I don't know about other progress, but it's very difficult to make progress on anything else!

Wendy: Because you can't keep your balance or your center when you're in a romance?

Simon: *(sounding frustrated)* Yes! Exactly! I can't work, I can't write, I can't do sports, things like have children – I just can't seem to do anything else.

Wendy: *(calmly)* So you make choices.

Simon: You have to be really, really absorbed in the relationship or it tanks.

Wendy: *(briskly, preparing to change topics – she would deal with her own emotions later as to why she had contracted with him for the romance of her lifetime?)* Okay. This is helpful for you to know. Thank you. We have a new question for your Higher Self. I would like the Higher Self to come in even more strongly and to stay with us. I'm requesting your Guides and the Light raise the vibration in the room for you and *to hold it steady*.

(pause)

Wendy: Have you met the two missing members of your soul group in this lifetime? Are you meant to know who they are?

Simon: Something is developing, but it's coming out very slowly.

Wendy: Take all the time you need, and know that you can understand it very clearly.

(pause)

Simon: Ask the question again.

Wendy: Have you met the two members of your soul group this life that you have not been able to identify previously, but believe exist?

(pause)

Simon: That's a tough one. I get the impression I have, but no revelation as to who they are.

(She chose to let it go for the moment, as he was tiring.)

Wendy: That's okay. You can just let it be, and know that much more info will come to you after this session – you will have dreams, you will experience more "just knowing" moments, you will have those little chance encounters that are very meaningful.

(pause)

Wendy: Trust your gut – you've got an excellent gut – listen to your audio recording – call in your Guides – set the table for them – it will come to you! Today's just the beginning for your doing this type of work for yourself very powerfully.

(no reply)

Wendy: Next question for your Higher Self. Has he had contact with Extra-Terrestrials?

(pause – vibration and feel of wisdom in the room went up)

Higher Self: Well, he hasn't in the sense of what you see in the movies or on TV. Not that at all.

Wendy: (smiling) Understand. It's often quite different than how it's portrayed in the media – a

62

lot more subtle. Then how do we resolve his feeling more tired some days when he gets up in the

morning than when he went to bed? He seems to sleep peacefully and doesn't snore, yet described it as feeling "worked over" and is having some severe lower back and kidney pain. He asked specifically if low vibration ETs could be involved.

(no reply)

Wendy: Who or what is causing this, and why? We need clarity on this.

(no reply)

Wendy: What's occurring? Are low vibration ETs involved? Do we need to establish his sovereignty?

(no reply)

(She spoke again firmly – prepared to clear his energy with his Higher Self and Guides, if needed.)

Wendy: You have the right to be sovereign in your own energy field and not to have any other energy aboard, including any ETs. That is Universal Law! You are a sovereign being. We all are. You are completely loved and protected by the Divine.

(no reply)

Wendy: Do we need to do some clearing work? This requires clarity NOW.

(long pause)

Higher Self: Hmmm...it looks like unresolved tension. His To-Do lists are too lengthy. Choices are not being made...

Wendy: *(relaxing in her seat)* Okay, how do we best resolve that? Is he working himself over, so to speak?

(Higher Self switches back to Simon.)

Simon: That was one of the purposes of seeing that first life – that bloke with the arrows – he had no such tension.

Wendy: Yes, Manfred the Huntsman?

Simon: Yes. It was a simpler life.

Wendy: And one with a lot of freedom?

Simon: Yes, freedom. He didn't have a smorgasbord of choices that had to be resolved. It seems like the two are being contrasted – my current life choice, and then.

(No longer speaking about himself in third person as Higher Self would do.)

Wendy: Yes?

Simon: If you want all that busyness, all that activity, all those options, all those choices, then the weighing and sifting of it is going to grate on you. It's going to work you over.

Wendy: So now that you know that, can you make a different choice?

Simon: It's not one choice. It's many choices.

Wendy: Well, now that you've been shown this information, are there new pathways or resolutions available to you?

Simon: Hmmmm. I don't know how to interpret it.

Wendy: *(firmly)* What is the Higher Self showing you? Please share the images immediately as you receive them, without interpretation or filtering. Your Guides are all with us. You have a full house here right now to help you.

(long pause)

Simon: Targets. Like targets opening and closing, opening and closing...

Wendy: What do the targets represent for you? I'm not meant to interpret. You need to do so for yourself. Who can best interpret this for you?

Simon: *(expressing frustration)* There's obviously nobody there! I'm not getting anything.

Wendy: *(briskly)* There is always someone there. We are always connected to and supported by the Divine.

(Long pause. Simon's energy felt sulky to her.)

Wendy: *(taking a risk – speaking very firmly)* You are past this point, *(name deleted)*! You now know how to call in your Guides – you set the table for them yourself just a few moments ago. Let's get this done NOW!

(long pause – no reply)

Wendy: *(calmly)* This is meant to come to you later then, when you listen to your MP3. Your recording is going to be so important, so very helpful to you.

(Neither of them realizes, ironically, his MP3 recording will be blank.)

(no reply)

Wendy: Next question. What is the purpose of your drive to write?

Simon: To find myself. What has been accumulated in a form so that I can maximize it, absorb it and share it.

Wendy: Very good. Tell me more why writing is so important for you?

(Vibration rises, as Higher Self comes back in with its great wisdom and calm.)

Higher Self: It's like he's story-telling on a grand scale. It's not around a campfire.

Wendy: On a grand scale, meaning *(example deleted)*, or his publishing his writing to share it with all interested audiences?

Higher Self: It wouldn't be just *(example deleted)*, it's his writing in general.

Wendy: *(nodding)* Okay.

Higher Self: Here's another example for him. Travel.

(pause)

Simon: *(switching back to first person)* I know there are those who experience things vicariously through me because they can't travel overseas themselves.

(pause)

Simon: I'm like the wagon-master in that way. That's something you've experienced.

(Likely referring to her past life as Oregon Wagon Train Leader Jesse Applegate.)

Wendy: Yes.

Simon: You, like me, know how to be out front. Not everyone can be out front.

Wendy: *(nodding)* Right.

Simon: Not everyone can be out front at once, either. It's not wise to do that. You can only have one wagon-leader at a time for a group. The wagon-master. The group leader...

Wendy: Agreed.

Simon: And somebody's got to be out front to see the landscape, and to describe it. To lay out a path. So the herd gets safely from here to there.

Wendy: Understand. What else?

Simon: We both know how to do that well. Sometimes we do it together.

Wendy: *(smiling)* Yes, we do. I'm grateful for many of the experiences we've shared and progress we've made together. Thank you! Let's get back to you.

(Switching gears to focus him more specifically on his session work.)

Wendy: What is your primary purpose in this lifetime?

(long pause)

Higher Self: *(switching back to third person)* Hmmm...it seems like it's for him to have a vast array of experiences. It's to balance up previous lifetimes where it's been very limited, with narrow-focused objectives or experiences. This time is to put together a whole picnic. A whole cornucopia...

Wendy: So he's balancing out, because we need to have all different types of lives to progress?

Simon: I don't know if it's balancing out. It's more fullness. The ones I've seen, the ones I've heard about from others. Living as a monk, for example, who couldn't speak? That's really limiting.

(Likely referring to their series of three silent monastery lives.)

Simon: Living in a wheelchair and being completely limited, in a physical way. Living as a Huntsman. All those seem very simple and not very involved, and not requiring a lot.

Wendy: Yet we're always learning through any experience. There are rest lives and reward lives, as you know – we plan our lives carefully. Anything else?

Higher Self: Those just require you to be there. His current life is very busy – very involved.

Wendy: *(nodding vehemently, remembering how difficult it had been to synch schedules when they were dating)* Yes, it is.

(Pause as she consults the list of questions he submitted before his session.)

Wendy: Would the Higher Self like to confirm a past life as King Arthur?

Higher Self: *(jokingly)* His Higher Self would like to hear an answer!

(Note: It's a sign of an excellent level of trance when a client refers to themselves in the third person – "his" Higher Self.)

Wendy: The Higher Self can do so now. Your Guides and the Light are all here – everyone is here for you, supporting you.

(long pause)

Wendy: Has this soul had a life as King Arthur of Camelot in England?

(long pause – sense of vibration in room falling)

Simon: No answer given.

Wendy: Additional insights will come to you later, then.

(pause)

Wendy: Has this soul had a life as William Shakespeare?

(pause)

Simon: That is stronger, but in each case it is more a matter of what we know about them. The archetype. We don't really know who William Shakespeare is. That's grey. We don't really know who King Arthur is. That's grey.

Wendy: *(firmly)* Why is it grey? It doesn't have to be unclear. You are in the Place of All Knowledge right now. Dial in! Find the information you need. You can access your own Book of Life in the Akashic Records yourself, or ask your Higher Self or Spirit Guide to bring it to you.

(long pause)

Simon: It's more like having a distinctive – very distinctive – hold on who the archetypes that each of those men represented, and being part of a collective mentality – there's a strong feeling that went into what we think we know about having been King Arthur or William Shakespeare.

(pause)

Simon: But having been a specific individual? Not so clear...

(pause)

Wendy: Thank you. Was your most recent past life as a Plantation Manager in the Pacific as you've been shown in a previous session?

Simon: No distinct answer I can hear, but I get a strong feeling of a yes.

Wendy: *(firmly)* Then it's a YES! Feeling or sensing are equally as valid as seeing or hearing or smelling or tasting, or just knowing. We have numerous clairs or psychic senses.

(no reply)

Wendy: Was the purpose to keep everything going for the good of the whole, or was there more?

(pause)

Simon: For me to be taken seriously, to be accepted and trusted unconditionally, I did my job sacrificially, so there would be no question.

Wendy: So that was his life lesson? To do that on behalf of the collective group?

Simon/ Higher Self: Yes.

Wendy: Thank you so much.

(pause)

Wendy: May we know whether his *(name and title deleted)* is in his primary soul group? Are we able to have those curtains open?

(pause)

Simon: That one's got a lot of shutters around it. It's going to need to be worked at.

(pause)

Wendy: *(letting it go as she sensed he was tiring)* All right. We will leave it for now. Know that more information will come to you easily, at the perfect time and place now that you have aligned with your Higher Self and Guides. You're doing great work!

(pause)

Wendy: Now that we are the deepest level where you can easily feel your connection to the Light, you can also know all the answers to your questions.

(Continues to give Simon guidance to assist him.)

Wendy: Why did you choose these lifetimes to explore? Is there anything additional to be spoken of now?

(pause)

Simon: Nothing is coming through.

Wendy: Very good. Then we know it is complete. It's time to confirm the healing of both the listed issues and any other ailments is complete. Did we heal everything permanently? Can the Light confirm that for us, please.

(no reply)

Wendy: Did the healing lights do all the work needed to heal him completely?

(long pause)

Simon: *(flatly)* No.

Wendy: *(working to mask her surprise)* No? What else needs to occur?

Simon: Some other type of healing needs to take place. Like knowing *why*. I need to know why all this neck and back pain. You didn't find the lifetime where this started.

Wendy: *(addressing the Light)* Let's go back to the original lifetime where the neck pain originated. He is very capable of doing that, and seeing clearly why this occurred, so he can leave the past, in the past.

(pause)

Wendy: He doesn't need to carry this pain – any pain – with him now. What can you, the Light, show us about that life to heal this now?

(long pause – sense of a major decision hanging in the balance)

Wendy: *(firmly – drawing her line in the sand)* We are not leaving this room until we fully heal his back and neck and knees. He can do this!

(no reply)

Wendy: *(taking her stand)* I have all day and all night, if necessary. It's time to heal and release, and to get his answers NOW!

(long weighty pause)

VIII: THE SUSPECT

(Important Note: This session was unusually graphic regarding the two lifetimes of origin that needed to be visited for Simon to receive physical healing for his neck, which he had broken and had surgically repaired, and to heal his back and knees.

If you are a High Sensitive or an Empath, you may wish to pause for a moment in order not to be unduly impacted. Then skim the next few pages with care, knowing everything written is necessary.

Do not be concerned you will ever experience anything you cannot handle if you have your own healing session of this type. You will be fully supported by your Higher Self, your Guides, and the Light, as well as by your Past Life Regressionist. You will be pulled up to the soul level to not feel trauma, and to gain a deep understanding as to what occurred in order to heal and release it permanently.)

Simon: Ummm *(shifting about uncomfortably)* Ummm...hmmm.

(She sent him Reiki healing energy.)

Wendy: *(gently)* What are you seeing in that lifetime – what are you experiencing? You're just fine now. Nothing is going to hurt you.

Simon: *(sounding miserable)* There's some sort of misunderstanding – like I'm a suspect. Only I'm just the wrong person – in the wrong place – at the wrong time!

(sound of him breathing heavily)

Simon: They didn't have trials then for that sort of thing. They didn't have lie detector tests. No due process. I may even have a handicap, like being deaf? Or dumb...

(Long pause – Wendy on high alert due to intense "crackling" type energy in room. She strengthened the White Light bubble of protection around each of them separately, and centered herself as she got a sense of the dungeons and wheels again from earlier.)

Simon: *(suddenly)* Oh, God, I'm being **racked**. I'm being racked!

(She intervenes immediately, knowing exactly what racking was. Racking was the most painful Medieval torture of all, used to slowly destroy joints and limbs.)

Wendy: Know that you don't need to experience any discomfort NOW. Or in this lifetime AT ALL. You can leave that experience in the past, and have wonderful health NOW, and ease and grace in your neck and shoulders and back now, in all of your strong, healthy body NOW.

(no reply)

Wendy: *(strongly)* That was then, and this is NOW! You don't need to carry this burden anymore. Let it go! You can heal and release this immediately.

(Weighty pause – sense of Simon considering her coaching. She continues to send him Reiki silently before speaking again, quietly and deliberately.)

Wendy: Is this resolved? There will be no more racking. That's done.

(Long pause. Simon cautiously moves his neck from side to side, and then stretches his back with the utmost of care.)

Simon: It feels much better now. How did you do that? It's way better. Amazingly better.

(pause as he continues to stretch gingerly)

Simon: But I don't know that it's completely resolved.

Wendy: *(briskly)* It can be. Let's resolve this right now. You are healing yourself with the Light! We're all here to help you. What was the healing color for your neck? Was it the orange you saw at the end of your work with the healing lights? Can that color come back in, and heal your neck now. Your neck doesn't need to cause you discomfort any more.

(Long pause – sense of Simon paying strict attention.)

Wendy: You're not broken in any sense of the word. You are unbroken. You are healed! You are healthy and happy in your strong body. You're a very active, strong athletic man. We have healed and released this –

Simon: *(interrupting)* Gold – I see the color gold.

Wendy: Fantastic! See that gold color healing you completely – see that gorgeous, powerful gold come back in – really see and feel it healing you – feel the warmth of it healing your neck, just like when you're outside on a perfect glorious, sunny day.

(Pause – sense of Simon weighing whether to heal, as it is ultimately his decision.)

Wendy: *(speaking calmly, with great determination)* I know you can feel the beautiful sun healing the back of your neck – feel it now healing your neck deeply, all the way down to the DNA cellular level. You don't need to feel that discomfort any more. That's done. It's over!

(pause)

Wendy: Is there anything further you need for your neck?

(pause)

Simon: Mmmm...I would say absolution for whatever part I may have played – whether deaf, dumb or blind – what originally led to this – there's betrayal in the mix – as you know – as you and I know together – we so know about betrayal!

(Possibly referring to their life at Camelot as King Arthur and Queen Guinevere, even though he only sees it as an archetype and isn't clear if he had that past life?)

Simon: *(speaking rapidly)* I just don't know the mix. Between being the wrong person, at the wrong place, at the wrong time – there's betrayal – it's complicated!

(He was becoming agitated.)

Wendy: *(soothingly)* That's okay. You're just fine now. You're healing it now. You can do this – we're all here with you. Just see and feel that amazing gold energy healing your neck. Bring in some royal purple or ruby red or any other color you need, too.

Simon: It's a cocktail – a terrible cocktail – in there somewhere, I may have complicated it and made it worse.

Wendy: Know that you can feel absolution – be free of any blame or guilt – feel forgiveness from the betrayal – you don't need to even understand it in your mind, give that part of you a rest – let it stand down – leave this in the past. Do it NOW!

(pause)

Wendy: *(testing for response)* Your neck is now completely comfortable.

(Simon adjusts position again, looking much more relaxed, but does not reply.)

Wendy: Is that the same lifetime that led to your problems with your tight upper back and shoulders and your back and kidney pain – was it the same experience we have just healed? Or is there a different lifetime to find to resolve to make your back perfect, too?

(pause)

(He sighed deeply several times, releasing more past life energy.)

Simon: There's a different lifetime – we need to find it – it's torture. It's definitely torture. We have to go there now.

(Wendy took a deep breath to summon all her reserves. First a World War II early death at age 19 and now not one, but two, torture past lives? She thanked her Guides for telling her ahead this would be the most difficult session of her life. She was a High-High Sensitive. This was not easy for either of them.)

IX: FORGIVENESS

Wendy: *(gently)* You're okay. I'm right here with you. I won't leave you. You're safe, all your Guides and supporting cast are with you. We're going to find the lifetime and heal it completely right now. You're completely safe, and nothing is going to bother you physically or emotionally.

(no reply)

Wendy: This is going to be easy. We've got this one, and we're going to heal it completely! You can pull up and watch it from a distance, or speed up this movie reel to view it quickly. You are completely loved and supported at the soul level.

(sense of Simon listening intently)

Wendy: I'd like you to travel now to that lifetime - the original lifetime – that led to this discomfort with your back – your entire back, between the shoulder blades, your lower back – your whole strong, healthy back. Let the years drop away --you can de-age at the cellular level. Sixty – fifty – forty – thirty – you choose.

(no reply)

Wendy: You are moving easily to that lifetime NOW. We are going to leave the past in the past, and you can simply report what you see or experience.

(no reply)

Wendy: What do you see?

Simon: Lots of masonry arches.

Wendy: Okay. Are you building something?

Simon: No. That's just representing the city. Okay. Lots of – ummmm- *(shifting about)* – lots of darkness *(yawning repeatedly)* – cold. So cold. Ummm....hmmmm.

(pause)

Wendy: *(gently)* You can pull your blanket up – feel the warmth – the comfort – the safety. What's happening now – what do you see?

Simon: Somebody is swearing at me. It's really, really bitter.

Wendy: You're just fine now. Where are they?

Simon: They're down below me. Looking up – I see a finger wagging. It's very hateful. Mmmm...

(Yawning deeply and repeatedly – sign of a major energetic release.)

Wendy: You're doing so well. You're an exceptionally strong, brave man, and one who is very loved and supported by the Divine. You don't need to experience discomfort of any type.

(no reply)

Wendy: You can pull up and watch this like an observer – pull back. Take a giant step back! You're safe. Watch it like a movie. You can make the screen small if you like, and still see clearly.

Simon: Mmmmm. *(shifting about)* Ohhh... *(yawning hugely)* I'm being bound, and being dropped. Dropped onto something...

(Yawning even more hugely as he released the past life energy.)

Wendy: *(calmly)* What are you being dropped onto? This won't cause you any discomfort. You're just the reporter – pull up and be the dispassionate reporter. Distance yourself and tell me what you're experiencing, *without feeling it*. Strengthen the White Light protection around yourself now.

Simon: *(reporting much more calmly)* Okay. It's something that won't stab me, but will break me. It's like a pointed rock – a pointed something? You see?

Wendy: *(flinching)* Yes, I understand. You're okay. Just be the reporter.

Simon: *(stoically)* It's to break you, not to stab you. You're not to go easy, you understand?

(She began crying silently, but kept her control.)

Wendy: Yes, I understand. You're just fine now. We are healing this right NOW! This was a long time ago. You don't need to carry this energy in your body any more. Let it go! It's time to heal and release this immediately. Right NOW. Now – Now!

Simon: It's calculated – you get pummeled. Torture. More torture.

Wendy: I understand. We are now going to move very quickly through this and heal it for good. We don't need to experience any more of this. I want you to move forward in time NOW! Follow my instruction. It's time for you to heal.

Simon: *(ignoring her)* You just get pummeled. It makes you bleed internally – and bruise.

(She changed tactics, realizing he was not likely to follow strong instruction from her – he would more likely battle with her even if it meant a poor outcome for himself of not healing. She changed her approach as this highly independent, extremely intelligent man needed to provide his own solutions.)

Wendy: *(working to sound blasé; shrugging to feign disinterest)* So how do we use this experience to heal your back? This is just powerful knowledge for healing. Is simply knowing this new information and understanding that you can leave this old energy in the past sufficient to fully heal now?

(long pause)

Wendy: *(calmly)* What do you need to heal this completely now? No more torturing will occur. We are healing this right NOW!

(no reply)

Wendy: You're the very picture of health and wellness. It's time to heal, and to de-age.

Simon: *(shifting about)* Mmmmm...

(pause)

(Sounds of Simon breathing hard.)

Simon: Maybe I need to forgive whoever did this. Maybe I never forgave them.

(Vibration in room rises rapidly – sense of more Light coming in.)

Higher Self/ the Light: We both need to forgive – this message is for both of us, you know – I never forgave them. It cost me, just like you didn't forgive me and it cost you when you became a ghost for hundreds of years after we were at Plimoth together.

(She blinked hard in surprise. Simon had leapfrogged to a different past life they shared to draw a parallel. In the 1600s he had been the well-known English Sea Captain William Pierce. He brought her from England as Ann Warren (along with her stepmother and four sisters) to reunite with her father Richard at Plimoth Plantation. Her father had emigrated on the Mayflower in 1620 to what is now Massachusetts.

Ann had recognized William Pierce as her primary soul mate during that three-month journey, though she was only a twelve-year-old girl at the time. She misunderstood from the relationship they had over the next five years that she and William were to marry when she was "just a little older." Ann never understood why he suddenly disappeared from her life just before her eighteenth birthday. She felt abandoned and utterly heartbroken, especially as her father had died suddenly a few weeks earlier.

Ann didn't understand until three hundred years later as Wendy (during her own hypnotherapy session) that Captain Pierce was already married with children that lifetime. He was never free to be with her. She was heartbroken and angry as she felt William Pierce had risked her reputation, and played her for a fool.

Ann recovered sufficiently to marry a much more compatible new love four years later. She was very happy with her barrister husband Thomas Little for more than thirty years, and they had a large family together. Thomas passed on suddenly when Ann was in her sixties, and King Philips' War broke out soon after Thomas' death. Ann was killed unexpectedly by an Indian arrow in the lower left side of her abdomen when she went out on her porch early one morning to let her cat in.

She dropped her body in 1676, but did not go Home. Ann waited for her beloved primary soul mate William as he had told her, "I'll be back for you." Due to a combination of her sudden painful death, confusion, unrealistic romantic expectations, and epic stubbornness at the soul level, Ann became an Earth-bound energy – more commonly known as a ghost – for over 300 years.

Wendy and Simon (formerly Captain Pierce) were finally able to send Ann – the ghost of her past life self – to the Light. Simon needed to first publicly recognize Ann (via Wendy) at a large gathering, to apologize, and to tell her how much he had cared for Ann. Ann – an aspect of Wendy's soul – finally had the closure she had so desperately craved, and Wendy was able to do the soul retrieval back into the appropriate part of her timeline.)

Regression Healing I

There was a long pause as Wendy processed this message from Simon's Higher Self and the Light, and how to use this information to help Simon.

Wendy: *(slowly at first, then animatedly)* Yes, it cost me dearly to be a ghost for so long! Some of our discordant energy from previous lives made me anxious as could be in our relationship, among other things.

(no reply)

Wendy: But we're both stubborn cusses, aren't we? Stubborn and STRONG! Use that strength NOW, *(name deleted)* and let's take care of business – it's time to heal and release this NOW!

(no reply)

(She unconsciously crossed her arms, narrowed her eyes, and raised her chin.)

Wendy: I'm not moving from this chair until you do so.

(no reply)

Wendy: Enough with this torturing each other – enough with this cat and mouse! It's over. It's done. C'est fini!

(no reply)

Wendy: *(changing tactics to speak more gently as she felt his resistance)* We are completing our last lesson together peacefully, right here and right now.

(long pause)

Simon: *(coyly)* You're stubborn as hell.

(Long pause – sense of him waiting to time his next remark perfectly.)

Simon: I, on the other hand, am perfect!

Wendy: *(laughing heartily)* So glad we have that on record!

Simon: We don't need it on tape. It's been chiseled in stone.

Wendy: *(archly)* I note *you* were being chiseled on stone. Are we done with that torture nonsense, so you can be the picture of health?

(no reply)

Wendy: *(appealing to his strong drive to achieve)* After all, you're perfect. So let's move to perfect health for you – you can choose it right now!

(Long pause while Simon chooses if he will heal himself.)

Wendy: Show me what you can do to heal your back and neck. Show me what you've got, and show it to me now!

(pause)

Simon: *(chuckling gently)* You're right – I am chiseled by stone.

(Wendy felt a huge sense of relief as a heavy weight come off her own shoulders and painful neck. She had whiplash in two separate car accidents, plus major back surgery as a teen. She saw Sisyphus stop endlessly, painfully roll his heavy boulder up the mountaintop only to have it roll down again as his eternal punishment.)

Wendy: So let's finish this cleanly. Clearly this is about forgiveness. We've moved through the betrayal and trust lessons. *Let's focus on forgiveness.* I forgive you, and you forgive me. Forgiveness transmutes karma, and is a path to freedom and ascension, among other things.

(no reply)

Wendy: Let's focus on you. Is forgiveness a gift to the person who harmed you, or is it a gift to yourself?

(pause)

Simon: Hmmm. Both. It's a gift to them both. It's a release for me.

Wendy: *(strongly)* Fantastic! That's a powerful realization. Are you ready to feel ease and grace in your strong, healthy body now? Are you ready to release all your back and neck pain, and leave the past in the past? Are you ready to release your knee pain, and any other pain anywhere in your body? The discomfort was just a useful tool to remind you of the past so we can heal it today.

(Sense of Simon considering her words carefully.)

Simon: Keep going – keeping talking in that vein – that helps me...

Wendy: The physical discomfort was just a gift to remind you of the life of origin of the issue, and now we have released it. Do you need more healing lights brought in? How do we complete this here and now, for good.

(no reply)

Wendy: *(gently)* How do we forgive? Do you need more Reiki from me? More healing lights? What do you need?

(no reply)

Wendy: Or is it already done?

(pause)

Simon: *(moving gingerly)* I don't know that it's all gone yet. The pain is not completely gone, but it's much better. I feel something shifting away from me – like it's leaving me.

Wendy: Perfect. You're spot on. That's the old energy leaving your body and your energy field. We will check back and make sure the pain is gone. Sometimes healing is instantaneous, and sometimes it takes a few days. Know that we've GOT this one! I recommend you drink a lot of water over the next few days to flush out this old energy.

(She suddenly was parched at the mention of water, and gulped down almost half the bottle of her own water. They were both clearing old energies very powerfully.)

Wendy: *(briskly)* You are very capable of this work – remember what you said about the need for forgiveness? That's your key to release this.

(pause)

Wendy: Do we need to return to a lifetime to heal your knees or anything else?

Simon: No. It's all about my back and neck. My broken neck.

(pause)

Wendy: *(frowning – reframing; asking his Guides to help him accept the reframe)* Your healthy, strong, flexible neck. You're as strong as an ox! No victims here.

Simon: Hmmm...

Wendy: What are you seeing?

Simon: I wonder who that is – do I know them now? It would help me to know who I'm forgiving – are they in my life now?

Wendy: *(strongly)* Who do you see? You are with the Light – you are with your Guides – everything can be made clear to you immediately. You can know the answer to any question in the Universe right now! I'm helping hold the energy and the light for you to release this.

(long pause – no reply)

Wendy: Get it done, *(name deleted)*! Who is the person who tortured you and dropped you – bound you and dropped you in such a punishing way – hurting your back? Who was that person?

(She missed his reference to there being more than one person who tortured him.)

Simon: Hmmm.

(There was a long pause in which he shifted about restlessly.)

Simon: *(quietly, sounding regretful)* It feels like it was my Mom.

(Wendy startled a bit, and had to work hard to control her voice to hide her surprise. She had expected him to perhaps name one of the two members of his soul group he kept asking about but couldn't identify in his current life. She knew he was very close with his mother, but it was a complex relationship. Personally she loved his mother dearly, and knew they'd been sisters and best friends more than once in other lives.)

Wendy: *(gently)* Ahhh. It's okay. This was a long time ago. So you need to forgive your Mom?

89

Simon: *(sounding very left-brained again)* I don't have absolute clarity...

Wendy: *(interrupting before he became even more uncertain)* Know what you are being shown is correct! Trust that the key is to forgive your Mom -- know it is the right info. Trust what you are being shown. You can do this...trust!

(no reply)

Wendy: *(gently)* We're back to our lesson of Camelot, aren't we? Let's move from our betrayals and restore our trust – feel the forgiveness and the hope of that amazing life, and the incredible love. The absolute magic of that place and time. Avalon.

(long pause – no reply)

Wendy: Your Guides are saying forgiveness is the key to more than you can possibly know. Your lessons with your mother. Lessons with others, especially women. No wonder it's so hard for you to be in a romance and to have a balanced life. This old energy is keeping you very off-balance. Let's release it immediately. You can do this!

(no reply)

Wendy: Only you can choose how to forgive your mother – how to trust your mother now. It will change your life completely to release this energy. Otherwise how can you trust a mother figure? How can you trust females, if you have been tortured like this by your own mother? Let's clean this up STAT!

(pause)

Simon: I don't know how. I don't have an answer. I would like a revelation to heal this.

Wendy: Okay. We're going to find it right now. I would like your Higher Self, your Guides and the Light to show us more immediately, and with great clarity. I'm holding the space for you.

(pause)

Simon: The next layer is here. I'm digging down through it.

(long pause)

Simon: I'm getting the feeling you were complicit with my Mom.

(She recoiled back hard on her chair in surprise, having had no idea of this sobering possibility. Yet she heard the confirmation immediately from her Guides it was true. There was a long pause as she regrouped. Tears began streaming down her face.)

Wendy: *(sadly)* Well, that would fit with the work we did at Camelot, wouldn't it? We've had to learn to heal betrayal, to learn to trust each other again, to learn to love again, and to learn to fully forgive. It would fit with our journey this lifetime to heal all that – we played it out again and again, in multiple lives.

(pause)

Wendy: Betrayal – trust – forgiveness. It's been staring us in the face, hasn't it? Let's finish it.

(no reply)

Wendy: *(working hard to keep her energy and voice steady and calm)* You told me you couldn't trust me when we broke up. You accused me of betraying you because of a dream you had of a woman who...*(details deleted).*

(pause)

Wendy: *(sadly)* I interpreted that dream very differently when we had dream synchronicity and dreamed the same dream the same night back when we were together. Even if I betrayed you, I know it was old energy, as I'm extremely trustworthy now.

Simon: Yes.

Wendy: We just couldn't fix it in time. We broke up instead, which we learned over time was best for both of us, despite our soul contract to be together, and my profound heartbreak when we broke up. Plus our romance contract was a snarled mess – we were working different versions of it. And some of our core values are too different this lifetime for us to be happy together long-term.

(pause)

Simon: *(nodding)* Yes. That's all true.

Wendy: *(tears continuing to stream down her face)* It's been a damned hard path we've walked side-by-side, *(name deleted)*. We've walked a challenging path together, though there was a lot of love and laughter and joy, too. We've both moved up as a result of all these amazing experiences together.

(no reply)

Wendy: *(crying hard)* I'm so incredibly sorry. I'm humbly asking for your forgiveness for ANY lifetime I've ever hurt you. I am down on my knees at your feet, bowing my head.

(pause)

Simon: Makes sense. Camelot, and much more.

(pause)

Wendy: *(quickly)* Camelot?

Simon: Yes. I see Camelot now, like you do.

Wendy: *(taking a deep breath)* Know that I forgive you for having me imprisoned in the nunnery, for playing me for a fool at Plimoth, for my broken heart with you this lifetime –

Simon: *(interrupting)* I now see Mom there clearly. But I *feel* your presence. I know your energy like the back of my hand. Even if it's something like being an advisor? You may not be hands-on. You may be the Inquisitor, or giving advice or something like that. You're a background player. But you're there! You're torturing me.

(long pause – she continued to cry silently)

Simon: That's it. You ARE the Inquisitor!

Wendy: I understand. I'm so terribly sorry. Please forgive me. This explains why I have been trying to heal your back and neck since we first met. I remember laying hands on you the first time we went to the movies, and your neck and shoulders and back were so painfully tight – oh, I see it now, it was from being racked.

(sounds of her quietly sobbing)

Wendy: That's how I knew what racking was, the second you said the word. That's why I stopped it so quickly. Some part of me knew...

(no reply)

Wendy: I'm so incredibly sorry, *(name deleted)*. Can you forgive me? What we've done to each other and with each other is profound. You've been there for so many of my highest highs and my lowest lows.

(no reply – sound of her blowing her nose)

Wendy: We soul mates play the most surprising roles in each other's lives, don't we? It's amazing how the roles change from lifetime to lifetime. So many lessons – such progress this lifetime! The critical question is how do we close this out in a healthy way?

(Long pause – sense of energy clearing in room, and vibration rising.)

Simon: *(sounding remarkably cheerful, upbeat and strong)* This should be easy! I think you know I'm pretty good at forgiveness.

Wendy: *(gratefully)* Yes, you are amazing at forgiveness. I'll never forget what you said to me a few years ago when Spirit pushed me so hard to ask your forgiveness for cuckolding you at Camelot with your best friend. You were so kind and open-minded to listen so respectfully to what likely sounded like such a long, out-there story from me.

(no reply)

Wendy: Do you remember what you said?

(pause)

Simon: Hmmm, I'm not sure? Remind me.

Wendy: We were outside *(restaurant name deleted)* by *(movie theater name deleted)*. You immediately said so cheerfully, "Oh, that's soooo 1,500 years ago! Don't even give it a second thought. I'm sure I've done the same or worse to you. Of course I forgive you. Just let it go."

Simon: *(cheerfully)* Yup, that sounds like me!

Wendy: *(gently)* One's mother is often the hardest person of all to forgive. She gives you the gift of life, and you expect her to always love and protect you.

94

Simon: *(nodding slowly)* Yes.

Wendy: You may be on your last round of forgiveness, to perfect that lesson. If you can't forgive your mother, multiple issues can arise, particularly in romantic relationships.

(no reply)

Wendy: Do you remember quizzing me about my relationship with my father when we first started dating? You were only interested in meeting a woman with a healthy relationship with her father. Yet I missed asking you about your mother...

(He nods.)

Wendy: Is there anything further that the Light and your Guides recommend for you to heal completely?

Simon: I need it to deliver what it can deliver now, and for you to show me how to do my part for after today. Teach me how to heal myself like you have. I really want to know!

(pause)

Simon: You're so much lighter. How did you do it?

Wendy: Thank you. I'd love to help you heal yourself. It's why we're here. There are lots of options. There's Reiki, which you're familiar with. Go for Reiki with our friends *(names deleted)* in person, or I can send you distance Reiki. There's also the green ray of healing, and there is the Violet Flame of transmutation. There are so many ways. You can use the Resurrection Flame where you regenerate your field, your energy, completely, and are born anew. Meditation helps you heal your crystalline DNA. It's why I keep recommending it for you. Go to a healing place as you fall asleep, and call in the healing lights to help you overnight. Listen to your MP3 and meditate more with the healing lights from today.

(no reply)

Wendy: I can teach you these ways to heal – I use them all myself, or I strongly encourage you to work with another healer if we simply have too much history. It's important you keep today's momentum going to heal yourself.

(no reply)

Wendy: You're familiar with all the varied sessions I've done with healers. You were incredibly kind to really listen with your heart to my many summaries, and to help me process through that storm of emotions. I know my healing sessions helped us both.

(no reply)

Wendy: You, more than any man in my life, have truly heard every word I've ever said to you, remembered our every conversation in all its nuance, and understood me deeply. I appreciate that more than I can fully express.

(no reply)

Wendy: I've been open in sharing my many healing sessions with you, *(name deleted)* as you were front and center in almost all of them, frankly, much more than I wanted you to be. I couldn't WAIT to have a session where you weren't mentioned! I wouldn't ask a single question about you, and there you'd be AGAIN, as vital to my healing as evidently I've been to yours. Today's the final step.

(no reply as he continued to listen intently)

Wendy: *(voice breaking)* We have so much history, but I had no idea of this piece of the puzzle until today. The cycle completes, *(name deleted)*. It's official. Your healer – your wife in many lives – your best friend – tortured you. Literally.

(no reply)

Wendy: I can only humbly ask for your forgiveness.

(no reply)

Wendy: And to give you mine for when the shoe has been on the other foot.

Simon: *(looking wiped out)* Ummm.

(There was a long pause as both needed to recover. She took a huge breath in after a few moments and quietly blew out all the old energy to focus on what he needed to heal. Clearly he first needed more energy to finish on a high note. He looked like he'd gone a few rounds with Muhammed Ali.)

X: RETURN TO THE LIGHT

Wendy: Here's what we're going to do. We're going to move more fully back into the Light. I'd like you to feel that energy, that bliss, the presence of the Light. Can you really feel that energy again – being Home, the unconditional love and peace, the endless support, no judgment – can you feel that?

Simon: It's easier when I visualize being Home.

Wendy: Perfect. You're wonderfully visual and you see, vs. feel. So be Home now. What do you see?

Simon: Hmmm.

Wendy: Are you back to your moonscape, or the winding paths?

Simon: *(shifting about)* Mmmm.

(yawning as he releases more energy)

Simon: Just skyscapes and light beams and moon beams and winding paths.

Wendy: Wonderful!

Simon: *(smiling)* Lots of great stuff! I see people's orbs.

Wendy: *(smiling in return)* Excellent. Know that you can experience Home anytime you need to. It will comfort and heal you. I am asking the Light to make that energy stronger for you so you know it's always present.

(pause)

Wendy: Is there anyone else you saw from your past lives that's present in your life now that you need to recognize?

Simon: No one else I recognize, but it certainly doesn't feel complete.

(pause)

Wendy: What else do you need to experience?

Simon: Hmmm...

Wendy: Is it incomplete because of the open questions around your *(identity deleted)*, and whoever else is in your soul group?

Simon: Well, yeah, that's part of it, but it's not all of it, though.

Wendy: What else feels incomplete?

Simon: *(Name deleted)* is not in my soul group. But she disappeared from my present life not long before you and I met and started going out. I'd like to know why. I know she and I have had past lives together, like you and I have. I know at one time – and I rarely do this – I had kids with her, with *(name deleted)*. It was like Medieval Italy? That life was confirmed in the reading I did with your friend Robin, the one where you helped hold the energy for me.

Wendy: *(nodding)* Yes. I remember.

Simon: As near as I can tell, I died as an artillery observer while covering the war. But she thought I abandoned her and the children. I didn't. I was just killed, and nobody cared. I was just another battlefield fatality. They don't exactly identify the bodies; they just cover you with dirt.

Wendy: So how can you best close that out with *(name deleted)* now in a peaceful way, so you don't have to experience it again? That's what today is for. Today is for taking care of all the old business! We are here to free you up.

Simon: I want to send her a message. I was there, I wanted to be there. I didn't – I didn't...

(pause)

Wendy: *(flatly)* You didn't abandon your wife and children that lifetime.

(She bit her tongue not to mention his many promises and then abandonment of her at Plimoth. That was off the table. Sessions were always for the client's behalf. This unique session had already been more about her than any other, and was utterly heart-wrenching at times. She had known before they began that morning that for him to have a successful session he needed to resolve the energy with the woman he considered the love of his life. She needed to help him do it for her own personal growth and freedom from him.

It was time for her to release the last of the anger and jealousy she still felt at times regarding his numerous romances with other women. His romantic interests were none of her business – they had transmuted their romance contract to be

100

together this life, and also the one to be primary soul mates. It was time for them to part peacefully, with love and gratitude for one another, and no regrets.)

(no reply)

Wendy: *(more gently)* Here is what we are going to do. You are going to connect with her Higher Self right now. Anyone can ask to connect with another soul's Higher Self at any time, incarnated or not, as we always have a portion of our energy at Home. I know you're familiar with that concept – you taught me.

(pause)

Wendy: This is one of many reasons I recommend you meditate. Even five to ten minutes a day when you're falling asleep or waking up would really help.

(pause)

Simon: *(humbly)* So what do I do?

Wendy: Just ask to speak with *(name deleted)'s* Higher Self, and tell her what you just told me. You can find her. Do it NOW.

(She dug deep to be generous to give him the maximum chance of success in his future romances. Wendy knew the former relationship he was referring to had been baggage when they were dating as he wasn't over his previous love. She'd had her own baggage, too. Neither of them had been able to "unpack" quickly enough, though both had tried with everything they had to be successful in their romance together.)

Simon: *(cautiously)* How exactly do I find her?

Wendy: *(more strongly)* Just connect through your heart. Put your hand over your heart to feel its beating, to feel the love. Just visualize her. She was the love of your life. Her Higher Self will hear you. Just tell her what happened. Do it now, while I hold the energy for you both with the Light. Make this right – use your strong telepathy skills NOW!

(Long pause – she held the energy well, and was able to feel serene for the first time regarding his love for the other woman.)

Simon: Hmmm. Okay.

Wendy: Very good. It's done!

Simon: I'm so tired...

Wendy: *(with empathy)* I know. I'm asking for more energy for you right now. I am going to finish speaking to the Light for you, and we are going to wrap up quickly.

(pause)

Wendy: Are there any additional lessons for him to learn from having lived as Robert, the solider who died in Italy during WWII, as that's the life he crossed over from?

(pause)

Simon: *(energy immediately returning)* It seems like we could have been interchangeable parts. It could have been any of us. It's just what we were to each other. We were bonded. It could have been me that got shot like it went down – it could have been anybody.

Wendy: Yes?

Simon: It didn't make a difference. You fall off a cliff, you get shot, you get betrayed. You get shot in a war, you get taken out as an impetuous Indian *(perhaps referring to their shared lifetime where she had been the tribe's Medicine Woman?)*, you die as a Ship's Captain from Spanish gunfire...

(Likely referring to Captain William Pierce, who died a hero saving his passengers and crew in the West Indies.)

(pause)

Simon: You get beheaded as a pirate.

Wendy: Yes?

(long pause)

Simon: Wait – I can't remember – you were there. Was I hung or beheaded that time?

(She quickly considers if this is another life that led to his current neck pain. She chose to summarize it for him as clearly he was not getting confused as to time and place as he continued to rattle off lifetime after lifetime of his, of hers, and of many they had shared.)

Wendy: *(sadly)* We saw you beheaded as Pirate King *(name deleted)*. I was your wife *(name deleted)*, and your mother was my older sister that lifetime.

(no reply)

Wendy: We were huddled together in the back of the town square to send you all our love and support. We were praying for the miracle of an escape or a pardon for all of you. Our only "crime" was bringing affordable food to the people. I'd do it again in a heartbeat!

Simon: Me, too. I have no regrets.

Wendy: *(quietly)* Nor do I. It tore our hearts out to watch you, my husband, and all the crew – all our closest friends, including my sister's lover, be brutally beheaded. We wanted to die, too. It would have been so much easier.

Simon: *(stoically)* How we die doesn't make any difference.

Wendy: What doesn't make any difference, the method of dropping your body, because you go Home regardless? Tell me more.

Simon: I'm not sure why we have different ways to end it each time. You never die the same way twice.

Wendy: *(working to lighten the mood)* That sounds like a James Bond movie. "Never Say Die!" or was it "Live and Let Die!"

Simon: *(smiling)* Yeah. Both.

Wendy: Perhaps it's because the soul craves experiences?

Simon: Well, the soul clearly craves experiences, but why do we die in such different ways? I'm not sure what comes from that. It's still dying.

Wendy: Perhaps it's a different experience because the soul craves experiences in order to progress, to grow, to move up in vibration. Why do you feel you drop your body a different way each time? What does the Higher Self say? You're not really dying – you know full well you're an eternal soul.

Simon: Yes. Our souls are immortal.

Wendy: Exactly. It's a different experience to have a lovely death with all your loved ones around you, and your bed pulled up so you are snuggled up to the fire, and it's as easy as can be.

(no reply)

Wendy: *(referring to one of her own deaths)* There's also the easy-peasy death where the Angels pull you out of your body and you exclaim, "YES! How wonderful. Please get me to my beloved now; I can't wait to see him." There's every possible experience.

(no reply)

Wendy: You can choose easier deaths, you know.

Simon: I guess, yeah, that's all true, but it's also an experience to die cold and miserable and alone. Or abandoned. Or slowly over time. I had one of those in the desert. Three days. Indian lance through my back. We must learn something new from each of those?

Wendy: Yes, we do.

Simon: We don't always see what it is at the time, though. Not until later.

Wendy: Correct. We understand it at Home as we debrief, as you know. We can ask more when you connect more fully with the Light. Let's go there now because I have some requests for the Light on your behalf and I know you are running out of steam. I see your restlessness, so we are going to finish your profound, amazing work quickly now. You can do this, so just stay with me! Can the Light...

(Session continued with requests to the Light on his behalf.)

Excerpts below with Simon's most pertinent comments –

Wendy: Can the Light give you guidance and messages clearly in your dreams?

Simon: And see that I am able to understand them.

Wendy: Yes, we are asking for you to remember and understand your dreams easily.

Simon: Good.

Wendy: Can the Light give you guidance and strength so you know you are never alone? Can you allow *(name deleted)* to feel that energy right now so he imprints it. Or so he sees it clearly. He's visual, but he's certainly capable of feeling, of hearing – we all have all our senses.

(pause)

Simon: Ummm... *(shifting about)* Wait...I **feel** something!

Wendy: *(crisply)* Fantastic! Imprint that – remember it always – you can dial right back into that any time you need it. This has been a major block for you and it's now removed! One of our primary purposes today was for you to heal enough to be willing to feel, and to align you with your Higher Self and your Guides. I can't believe how much you've done today.

(no reply)

Wendy: Is there anything that needs to be done to prevent the ailments from returning?

Simon: Hmmm...

(repositioning himself more comfortably, no further reply)

Wendy: Are there any higher dimensional beings working with you in addition to the five Spirit Guides we're aware of?

(long pause)

Simon: Archangel Michael.

Wendy: Wonderful, very good! So you may see a blue light around you at times, which is often a sign of Archangel Michael. Know too that Archangel Michael is amazing at cutting cords of attachment, karmic cords once the lesson has been learned, which often includes forgiveness. You may request he do that for you.

(no reply)

Wendy: Can you heal and release *(name deleted)* from any karmic connections that no longer serve him in a positive way this lifetime?

(He was shifting about uncomfortably. She heard from Spirit to move him along as quickly as possible.)

Simon: Oh, God.

Wendy: Can the Light heal and release *(name deleted)* from any karmic bonds that no longer serve him this lifetime? He may have more cords in addition to the many we've transmuted between us.

Simon: Ummm. Ummm...

Wendy: Will the Light answer us regarding the karmic bonds that don't serve him?

Simon: *(sound frustrated)* The Light isn't answering me. It seems to be saying YES, when it joins in.

Wendy: *(calmly)* Then it's a yes! Please go with the flow of the beneficial healing energy you're feeling.

Let it carry you Home to perfect health and more. You're bucking the tide. This will be life-changing for you. We ask the Light to bestow on *(name deleted)* the true power of forgiveness, for himself and for others.

(no reply)

Wendy: Is that appropriate. Will that be granted?

(Vibration in room increased.)

Simon: *(strongly)* Yes!

Wendy: Wonderful! We are very grateful. It's why we came here today. Is *(name deleted)* sovereign – does he have only his own energy board? Can he protect and clear his own energy when necessary?

(no reply)

Wendy: He feels extremely grounded. I used to ground from him until I learned to ground for myself. We all must ground for ourselves. Please verify he is free of other energy that's not his own.

Simon: *(nodding)* Strong yes! I hear a very strong yes. I'm completely sovereign.

Wendy: Perfect! So there is no issue with his kidneys being tapped by other energies – his back and kidney pain is resolved from the lifetime where his back was harmed and he learned forgiveness?

(pause)

Simon: Yes.

Wendy: Wonderful! We're so very, very grateful. Do you, the Light, have any final message for *(name deleted)*?

(long pause)

Simon: I hear just keep doing the work.

Wendy: Very good. I know you're tired from your amazing work today, so we're going to wrap up. Would you like to do this work again?

Simon: *(considering)* Yes – I think I would. Yes.

Wendy: Super. Then you can choose a key word to use for the future. It will make your trance level much deeper and more consistent, and help you reach therapeutic trance level more quickly than we did today.

Simon selected a keyword to use in the future with any Regression Healing or Quantum Healing Practitioner. Their intense session was concluded and debriefed.

The Past Life Regression was so unusually emotional for Wendy that when Simon joined her in his living room after the session, he found her squatting low on the floor with both palms flat as she worked to ground back to the magnetic core of Mother Earth. Wendy's energy was completely out of her body from the immense effort it had taken to help Simon connect and to stay connected for so long. He had been right to tell her he had trouble sustaining a therapeutic level of trance.

She wasn't yet able to walk outside, to take her shoes off and to ground properly in the grass. Both had worked so hard and released so much it took her several hours to fully come back into her body. It would be one of the last sessions she would do in person. Spirit guided her to move to doing healing sessions via Skype or teleconference. They would be equally effective for her clients from the start as she was a highly adept distance healer, and allowed her to meditate and to sleep immediately after the session if necessary to complete the healing process for both parties.

Simon and Wendy had finally healed and released their significant past-life history, with no regrets, and were able to celebrate their many lives together. Both had finally forgiven each other after thousands of years. And now Wendy would have to forgive herself for what she had done to him to share their story publicly. That took a year.

AUTHOR'S END NOTE

I was guided to look up what happened in world events in 1266. Why did the Lord High Mayor fight saying that date so hard? The energy was palpable with his resisting stating it. Perhaps it was another past life bubbling to the surface, but not yet ready to be released.

Feb 26th, 1266 – The Battle of Benevento was fought in Southern Italy between Manfred of Sicily and the army of Charles of Anjou.

Is it synchronicity that the first past-life name Simon found as "The Huntsman" was Manfred, his second past life as the French nobleman was set in 1266, and his past life as Robert, the nineteen-year-old World War II American soldier included landing at Sicily (Italy)?

Was his soul at the Battle of Benevento? Does he perhaps have a connection with Manfred of Sicily or Charles of Anjou?

I recommended Simon make a note to consider asking his Higher Self and Guides about this if he did a follow-up session as our best truth comes from within. All the answers we need are there.

Wendy Rose Williams

FORGIVENESS QUOTATIONS

"True forgiveness is when you can say *thank you* for that experience."
Oprah Winfrey

"The wisdom of forgiving: It does not mean giving people the license to hurt you over and over again. It is simply an act of releasing the pain others may have caused and remembering never to let them take away your peace again."
Dodinsky

"The weak can never forgive. Forgiveness is the attribute of the strong."
Mahatma Gandhi

"Forgiving isn't something you do for someone else. It's something you do for yourself. It's saying, 'You're not important enough to have a stranglehold on me.' It's saying, 'You don't get to trap me in the past. I am worthy of a future. I'm moving on to peace and happiness.'
Jodi Picoult

"We must develop and maintain the capacity to forgive. He who is devoid of the power to forgive is devoid of the power to love. There is some good in the worst of us and some evil in the best of us. When we discover this, we are less prone to hate our enemies."

Martin Luther King, Jr.

"Few suffer more than those who refuse to forgive themselves."

Mike Norton

"To forgive is to set a prisoner free and discover that the prisoner was you."

Lewis B. Smedes

"It's one of the greatest gifts you can give yourself, to forgive. Forgive everybody."

Maya Angelou

"The practice of forgiveness is our most important contribution to the healing of the world."

Marianne Williamson

FORGIVENESS RESOURCES & TECHNIQUES

What is your most effective forgiveness technique? Have you ever needed to "forgive the unforgivable" as depicted during Simon and Wendy's Regression Healing session? Were you able to do so?

What did truly forgiving do for you? What about the other person? Were you able to sense the freeing-up of energy that resulted from mastering the lesson?

Do you need to forgive yourself most of all? How can you be accountable for your actions, and still forgive yourself to heal your Inner Child and Shadow Self as needed? What will it take to love yourself without judgment, and to be your own beloved at all times? Do you have a "self" lesson to master, such as self-acceptance, self-love, self-respect, or self-confidence?

Here are a few of my favorite forgiveness techniques for inspiration. The person doesn't need to be currently in your life, or even to be incarnated in a body for powerful healing to occur.

Ho'oponopono Prayer

The ancient Hawaiian Ho'oponopono forgiveness prayer: "I love you, I'm sorry, please forgive me" is extremely powerful. It can be used as a mantra, ritual, technique or prayer.

Meditate Higher Self to Higher Self

We are all capable of meditating and clearing our minds, though it may take practice at first. Meditate and ask to connect with the other party's Higher Self. Connect from your heart space to theirs the best way you can. Declare your intent truly to hear them, and to resolve the issue(s) together in a peaceful manner. Have a loving conversation, reach the best agreement you can, and watch for the resulting miracle of new possibilities to present!

Peace Pipe Meditation

Meditate or pray to visualize smoking a peace pipe. Invite a person you are experiencing conflict with to join you. Connect with them Higher Self to Higher Self, with love and peace in your heart. Use the peace pipe to help you release your emotions fueling the conflict. They may include anger, frustration, impatience, resentment or jealousy, for example.

Visualize yourself smoking the peace pipe once for each emotion that's triggered by the other person. Blow out a single smoke ring, release it, and watch the emotion disappear into the ethers. Feel the peace and the freedom. Bless the emotion for what it taught you. Bless the other person as your teacher.

When you are complete, pass the peace pipe to your guest and invite him or her to do the same. Listen carefully to what has been triggering them in your interactions. When they are complete, thank them for the lessons and the opportunity to grow at the soul level.

Bow to each other or shake hands to end the ritual. Go forth in peace. If you are triggered again in the future or appear to be triggering the other individual, simply visualize the peace pipe and heal the energy with forgiveness and gratitude.

MAP Meditation

Machaelle Small Wright has created a simple yet powerful meditation technique called MAP – Medical Assistance Program. It involves asking the Divine for assistance in healing whatever is troubling you, being willing to receive the information and then to do the work to complete the lesson.

Wright's book "MAP: The Co-Creative White Brotherhood Medical Assistance Program" is available on Amazon. Don't be put off by the title as terms have changed since the book was published.

Wendy Rose Williams

WENDY'S HEALING PRACTITIONER RECOMMENDATIONS

My belief is we all benefit from a formal session with a healer from time-to-time. I have the privilege to work with the following practitioners personally. All have the utmost integrity, as well as a pristine connection with the Divine. Each is able to work via Skype, phone appointment and/ or email, and the healing and information is equally effective at a distance as face-to-face.

Robin Alexis is a Mystic, Reiki Healer, the "Metaphysical Mother," and so much more. Robin has had a phenomenally positive impact on my life. She is a world-renowned psychic, as well as co-host of the popular weekly healing program "Mystic Radio with Robin Alexis" with her husband and producer Bob Bordonaro.

See RobinAlexis.com

Matthew Bueno is a Master Energy Medium, metaphysical healer and teacher from the Yaqui and Aztec Nations. He is a Mt. Shasta, California Shaman, and is Robin and Bob's personal healer. Matthew's connection with the Ascended Masters and Angels is unparalleled.
See AscendedMasterAngels.com

Karen Downing is a spiritual teacher, author and channel. She provides a variety of one-on-one classes and personal mentoring programs designed to help you realize your soul's potential. Karen's accuracy, clarity and detail is extraordinary.
See YourSoulMission.com

Darcy Pariso is a psychic medium, animal communicator and Reiki Master. Darcy is the person I trust to do my own Reiki healing sessions and readings. She provides wonderful support and insights regarding my animal companions.
See DarcyPariso.com

Jude and Paul Ponton's healing treatments at Whispering Dragon include harmonic medicine, traditional Chinese medicine, chiropractic medicine and Acutonics sound healing treatments. Whispering Dragon offers remote property clearing and balancing services which are equally effective as their in-person services in Seattle, having experienced both.
See Whispering-Dragon.com

Laurie Regan is an Intuitive Artist and metaphysical author. She has drawn many of my past lives and her readings related to them have been incredibly helpful. I'm blessed to have Laurie's art in my home and to work together as writing partners.

See "Spirit Art by Laurie Belle" on Facebook
Email: LaurieRCreations@gmail.com

Valerie Shinn is an Intuitive Astrologer. The natal chart reading Valerie did for me was remarkably insightful. Services are quite affordable, especially if you don't know where to begin your spiritual journey, or are looking for your next step.

See ValerieShinn.com

Deborah Stelfox is a Spiritual Numerologist. Her comprehensive numerology reading was so stunningly accurate and detailed it literally changed my life. My reading with Deborah will be included in my upcoming "The Flow" trilogy to illustrate how a powerful reading can steer the course of your life in a more positive direction. She specializes in intuitive readings regarding karma and its antidotes.

Email: stelritz@foxinternet.net
Phone: 425-788-8187

I highly recommend both an astrology and a numerology reading for anyone working to raise their vibration. This powerful information allows you to progress both in your life now and in future incarnations.

Donya Wicken is a playwright and author of the upcoming book series "I'm Just an Ordinary Dead Guy." She and her partner Ben (who is on the other side) specialize in helping Earth-bound energy – stuck souls or ghosts – move to the Light.

I see this as a great service to humanity as souls can remain behind longer than they should, and then don't heal properly at Home. This can create anxiety and many other issues as the soul is fragmented when a soul retrieval is needed.

Perhaps you need help with some Ghost-Whispering to encourage a soul to move to the Light? Visit Donya's website TheZenofBen.com to understand this very real phenomenon.

My past life ghost experience as Ann Warren Little is linked below.

http://www.thezenofben.com/the-woman-who-haunted-herself

Consider a donation to TheZenofBen.com for their years of wonderful community service.

RECOMMENDED READING LIST

AFTERLIFE

Flipside: Tourist's Guide How to Navigate the Afterlife, by Richard Martini

(Look for Rich's 90-minute "Flipside" documentary on Amazon, too, as well as the book.)

It's a Wonderful Afterlife (Volumes 1 & 2), by Richard Martini

Hacking the Afterlife: Practical Advice from the Flipside, by Richard Martini

I have the pleasure of knowing filmmaker and author Rich Martini as a Facebook friend. I highly recommend his well-researched, thought-provoking books and documentary.

Heaven is for Real: A Little Boy's Astounding Story of His Trip to Heaven and Back, by Todd Burpo

Wendy Rose Williams

Proof of Heaven: A Neurosurgeon's Journey into the Afterlife, by Eben Alexander, MD

I thoroughly enjoyed meeting Dr. Alexander during his book tour to the Center for Spiritual Living in Seattle. He was so gracious in accepting a copy of Dr. Newton's "Journey of Souls" from me. I didn't know I was to give him my spare copy until I was standing in line for an autograph.

ASCENSION & VIBRATION

Frequency: The Power of Personal Vibration, by Penney Peirce

Peirce's premise is that our thoughts create our reality more powerfully and quickly than ever before. We truly are what we think, so must become masters of our thoughts as they manifest so quickly and powerfully. This is the "Law of Attraction" on steroids!

How to Raise Your Vibration, by Sabrina Reber

I highly recommend this powerful workbook available for sale, or at no charge on Sabrina's Facebook page. It includes an excellent chapter on forgiveness. You can do a keyword search for "forgiveness" in the electronic version of the workbook on Amazon.

Seven Sacred Flames, by Aurelia Louise Jones

This marvelous material has had a tremendous impact on my life. We studied it together in Robin Alexis' Soul Spa Book Club multiple times as it always has new insights to offer, particularly in

124

combination with Robin's unparalleled channeled updates. The Seven Sacred Flames is the only book I always keep on my night stand. The meditations to journey to the various etheric healing temples are gorgeous. Consider recording them to your phone or other device to listen as you meditate or fall asleep.

ANGELS & SPIRIT GUIDES

Assertiveness for Earth Angels: How to be Loving Instead of "Too Nice" and other titles by Doreen Virtue, PhD

Earth Angel is Doreen's term for Light workers. Doreen Virtue's "Healing with the Angels" oracle cards were how I first consciously connected with my Guides.

How to Meet & Work with Spirit Guides, by Ted Andrews

The Messengers: A True Story of Angelic Presence and the Return to the Age of Miracles, by Julia Ingram and G. W. Hardin

MISCELLANEOUS METAPHYSICAL

The Best of Spiritual Writers Network 2014 (multiple authors)

I am honored to have a short story included in this volume with my writing partner Laurie Regan. Laurie Regan's short stories are deceptively simple reading, yet are packed with wisdom and a tremendous love for humanity.

Look for Laurie's titles on Amazon:
The Edge of Hope
More than Meets the Eye: Tales of the Metaphysical
Visions Awakened: The Journey Continues
Lizzy
Stepping Through the Doorways of the Soul

The Emotion Code, by Bradley Nelson, DC

I was thrilled to learn how to muscle-test from this book to easily and accurately hear my Spirit Guides.

Emotional Freedom: Liberate Yourself from Negative Emotions and Transform Your Life, by Judith Orloff, MD

How to move from bitterness to forgiveness.

Heal Your Past Life Fears: A Guided Process to Reach Your Soul's Potential, by Ainslie MacLeod

MacLeod skillfully presents the top ten past-life fears holding people back, and provides the antidotes. I recommend an audio version as the best-selling author, highly respected psychic and hypnotherapist has a healing voice.

How to Talk To Your Dead Loved Ones in One Hour or Less, by Becky Buchko

My dear friend Becky makes the incredibly useful technique of communicating Higher Self to Higher Self to any soul straightforward, regardless if they are incarnated or not. Look for Becky's other titles, too, on Amazon.

Raising Humanity: Metaphysical Mothering is the Antidote to Terrorism, by Robin Alexis and various authors

Robin's Song, by Robin Alexis

Robin's unflinching, courageous autobiography brought me to tears more than once.

Robin's ebooks are available at no charge on her website at *RobinAlexis.com*, or for sale as print copies on Amazon. Consider making a donation to keep the long-running, self-funded "Mystic Radio" on-air if you download Robin's free ebook versions.

RELATIONSHIPS

The Brain in Love: Twelve Lessons to Enhance Your Love Life, by Daniel Amen, MD

The Female Brain, by Louann Brizendine, MD

The Male Brain, by Louann Brizendine, MD

Five Love Languages: The Secret to Love that Lasts, by Dr. Gary Chapman

This powerful little book can be used to enhance your relationship with anyone, not just a partner.

Passionate Marriage: Keeping Love Alive in Committed Relationships, by David Schnarch, PhD

You don't need to be married or even in a relationship to benefit from this gutsy material. I discovered and read it with much lively discussion with a boyfriend after our romance ended. Much healing ensued for us both.

Wendy Rose Williams

ABOUT THE AUTHOR

Wendy Rose Williams was born in Granby, Quebec, Canada, and lived in Florida, Atlanta, upstate New York and Boston before making her home in the Seattle area as of 1993. She is blessed with two amazing daughters, a supportive family and friend network, and a black cat named Midnight who is her faithful companion. Wendy has a profound memory for and understanding of past life energy.

Upcoming solo publications include "The Flow," a metaphysical fiction trilogy inspired by more than sixty of Wendy's past lives; additional Regression Healing™ client sessions in this series; and short stories on various metaphysical topics.

Wendy is co-authoring a universal life-force healing book with renowned Mystic Robin Alexis, host of the popular weekly "Mystic Radio with Robin Alexis" program. The universal healing information will be available as both a workbook and a teleconference course around the spring of 2017, with Robin and Wendy co-teaching the materials.

Training & Certifications

☐ Wendy works with Mystic Robin Alexis of Mt. Shasta, CA as her primary spiritual teacher. She has also worked extensively with Karen Downing, Jude Ponton, and most recently with Matthew Bueno.

☐ Certified as a Regression Healing Practitioner by Chris Turner, Quantum Healing Centre (West Wellow, United Kingdom)

☐ Reiki Levels I, II and III/ Reiki Master level training with Reiki Master Rus Sullivan (Dr. Mikao Usui lineage – Edmonds, Washington)

☐ Channeling Levels 101, 102, 103 and 104; Past Life Patterns; Learn About Your New Chakras and additional training with Karen Downing at Your Soul Mission (Issaquah, Washington)

☐ Mystic Radio Institute "Evolutionary Foundations Levels I and II" 8-week courses with Robin Alexis and Matthew Bueno

☐ Private Cosmic Coaching five-course series with Mt. Shasta Shaman Matthew Bueno

☐ Stargates International Meditation three-day retreat with Prageet Harris and Julieanne Conard (TheStargateExperience.com)

☐ "Frequency Shifting for Consciousness Expansion and Reality Creation" 2-day course with Jude & Paul Ponton (Whispering Dragon, Seattle, WA)

☐ Ordained Minister, Universal Life Church (Modesto, California)

ALSO BY THE AUTHOR

Wendy's first short story *"A Tiny Bow and Arrow"* won a writing contest. It was published in "The Best of Spiritual Writer's Network 2014: A Collection of Inspirational Short Stories and Poems" January 2015. The collection is available on Amazon.

Short Stories

"The Path to Forgiveness: Ramona Falls"

Can Jesse Applegate, Oregon Wagon Train Leader, learn to forgive himself for the many deaths that occur along the trail in 1843?

Email AuthorWendyRoseWilliams@hotmail.com to receive a FREE copy of this short story inspired by her past life pilgrimage to explore her past life as Jesse Applegate, the Oregon Wagon Train leader referred to by Simon during his session. It is another story illustrating the need for self-forgiveness.

"The Car Whisperer: Trust Your Intuition"

Gwen learns the hard way – and from a most unlikely teacher – to trust her intuition.

"Jack's Journey Home"

Can an elderly man who has suffered a severe head injury actually have been one of the Apostles?

WORKS IN PROGRESS

Metaphysical Fiction

Novels

"Prequel to The Flow: Plimoth Plantation"

Meet a heartbroken young female who refuses to go Home for over 300 years. Ann Warren Little shares her life story from her birth in England in 1611 to her lifetime and eventual death at Plimoth Plantation. What will it take to get this incredibly stubborn ghost to journey Home to the Light?

"The Flow I: Plimoth Plantation"

Gwendolyn Audrey Rose's "prescription" from her physician for on-line dating has startling results. She unintentionally manifests her primary and teaching soul mate, and discovers they share more than a dozen past lives as well as significant challenging karma. Their romance doesn't work in this lifetime as she wants it to, but Gwen can't let it go. She learns the ghosts of our past can be startlingly real.

Gwen becomes a spiritual seeker to progress, and alternately heals and releases or is uplifted and amused by her plethora of past lives. She suffers through the terror of two Dark Nights of the Soul and over time reconnects more deeply with her Spirit Guides, Angels, Ancestors and God.

Her life is transformed when a Mystic named Robin heals her with the indescribably beautiful White Light of the Universe, and gives Gwen the gift of a Reiki life-force energy attunement. She receives unconditional love, wisdom and support from many healers, family and friends.

Gwen surmounts significant pain and heartbreak during a wild roller coast ride to increase her soul energy vibration from 3D to 5D and higher. She learns we are all "Saints and Sinners," sense of humor is a life requirement, and John Lennon had it pitch-perfect: "Peace and love are eternal."

"The Flow II: Restoring the Divine Feminine"

Gwendolyn Rose begins to sense her true identity and purpose as she continues to spiritually awaken rapidly. Her life purpose includes restoring the balance between the Divine Feminine and the Divine Masculine. She continues to make past life pilgrimages to close out old energy that no longer serves her, and to master her soul-level lessons.

The painful implications of seeing another woman wearing the same unique necklace as Gwen's cause her to emotionally fall apart. She unexpectedly reunites with a beloved sister from 2,000 years ago when she gives a stranger her amber necklace gift that she can't bear to wear again herself.

Gwen begins to connect profoundly with Isis, Mary Magdalen, Mother Mary, Quan Yin and other representatives of the Divine Feminine. She receives critical assistance from a wide variety of healers on both sides of the Veil. Gwen is stunned to realize she is one of the souls who volunteered to bring Heaven to Earth in the form of the peace, love and joy energies.

"The Flow III: Mary Magdalen Remembers"

Gwendolyn Rose continues to experience a fast-paced, profound spiritual awakening. She is stunned by the scope and implications of her two hypnotherapy sessions in the summer of 2014. Three of Gwen's friends have their own separate sessions that same week. They agree not to discuss them until all are complete. Amazingly, all four women travel to critical points of intersection in Egypt and Jerusalem. Each confirms the other's identities in that lifetime often referred to as "The Greatest Mystery on Earth."

Gwen's memories during her comprehensive hypnotherapy sessions include the Egyptian Temple of Isis, one of the Mystery Schools. She reunites with her beloved two thousand years earlier as Mary at the well outside the temple, and they agree to marry. Mary is instead forced to marry John, a prophet for God, upon her return to Jerusalem. She is widowed by a barbarous act, and gifted a horrific item in an attempt to control her.

Mary reunites with her beloved a second time after her first husband John's death, and they marry. A decade later, her adored husband agrees to be taken by Roman soldiers to save mankind. Mary and her children escape by ship to Egypt after his most remarkable apparent death. A pregnant Mary and her son and daughter later settle in France. She raises her children alone, and begins to write her autobiography.

Three decades pass. Mary's final fear is not death, but can she finish writing her "Book of Love" before transitioning Home? And then will her story remain safely hidden until the time returns for it to become a gift to humanity?

Non-Fiction

Additional client sessions in the "Regression Healing" series

Universal healing life force workbook co-authored with Robin Alexis

Wendy Rose Williams

AUTHOR INTERVIEW LINKS

Wendy is grateful to have appeared on the following radio programs to discuss her energetic experiences including waking up spiritually, reincarnation and past lives, managing our energy fields, and raising our vibration to 5D (and higher) in order to experience profound peace, love, and joy.

She discussed her unexpected spiritual awakening and unusual introduction to Past-Life Regression and Life-Between-Lives spiritual regression with host Jason Havey on his 90-minute "Spinning Logic" podcast in October of 2015.

http://jasonhavey.com/267-2/

Jason had a Regression Healing session with Wendy in March of 2016. The following link is to their follow-up podcast regarding his session. It includes an interesting twist regarding potentially manifesting a future Near-Death Experience.

http://jasonhavey.com/spinning-logic-79-wendy-williams/

Wendy Rose Williams

Wendy was interviewed by Kimberly Thalken on Daily OM Radio's "Inspired Living with Marc and Kim" September 2016. Topics included Regression Healing, past lives, karma and soul contracts.

Their one-hour conversation is available as an MP3 or by searching YouTube.

http://s103.podbean.com/pb/e27e55d7470b5d8f19 63ff188feb8c92/57e58dde/data2/fs7/705661/ uploads/Inspired_Living-20160921.mp3

https://www.youtube.com/watch?v=FqhkNItPAFk

During 2015 Wendy was a guest multiple times on Chris Turner's "New Earth Radio" from the United Kingdom, on Katerina St. Claire's "Miracle Advantage Radio," and on Rich Vernadeau's "Daily Talk."

(Note: Wendy Williams recorded the 2015 interviews under the name Gwendolyn Rose.)

New Earth Radio with host Chris Turner 2/17/15 (46 minutes)

Topics: Past lives/ Past-Life Regression/ Quantum & Regression Healing

http://newearthradio.quantumhealingcentre.co.uk /radio/archives.html

New Earth Radio 5/9/15 (40 minutes)

Topic: The Role of Karma & How To Transmute It http://newearthradio.quantumhealingcentre.co.uk /radio/index.html

Regression Healing I

Daily Talk with host Rich Vernadeau 4/11/15
(1:46 minutes)

Topic: Reincarnation and Past Lives Role in
Progressing Spiritually

https://clyp.it/1nlo4bpo

Daily Talk with host Rich Vernadeau 9/19/15
(60 minutes)

Topic: How to Work with your Past Lives for a
Better Now

https://clyp.it/jb0313kz

Topic: "Metaphysical How-To Night: Connect with
your Guides; Enhance Your Meditation Practice;
Ground, Protect & Clear Your Energy; and Raise
Your Vibration to 5D and Beyond"

https://clyp.it/ycux1ucf

Miracle Advantage Radio with host Katerina St.
Claire 3/5/15 (1:08) Episode 13

Topics: Spiritual awakening, past lives, Past-Life
Regression, Life-Between-Lives

http://recordings.talkshoe.com/TC-136190/TS-
953135.mp3

Miracle Advantage Radio 3/14/15 (59 minutes)

Episode 14 (Part II from 3/5/15)

http://recordings.talkshoe.com/TC-136190/TS-
955825.mp3

Wendy Rose Williams

IMPORTANT DISCLAIMER

Wendy Rose Williams is not a Medical Doctor and does not prescribe medical treatment or dispense medical advice. You are advised to consult your own medical doctor or health-care practitioner for treatment. By law, only licensed medical practitioners can prescribe medical treatment in the United States of America.

Wendy is an Ordained Minister and Reiki Master healer whose sole desire, purpose and intent are to help others explore their spiritual nature to maximize their own emotional, mental and physical well-being.

Wendy does not provide guided meditation services to individuals diagnosed with schizophrenia, bi-polar disease, or Dissociative Identity Disorder (DID) as she is not a licensed medical or mental health professional.

In the event you choose to act on any of the information in this book, the author and publisher assume no responsibility for your actions.

Wendy Rose Williams

REGRESSION HEALING SESSION FREQUENTLY ASKED QUESTIONS

Q. What exactly is Regression Healing?

A. The Regression Healing technique is a guided meditation. Any hypnosis is self-hypnosis, and all healing is self-healing during this spiritual journey.

Q. What can I expect in a Regression Healing session?

A. Regression Healing sessions are designed to be an uplifting quantum experience for your soul. Your Higher Self, Guides and the Light can provide spiritual guidance in many areas, including your health, diet and lifestyle, relationships, parenting, career, life purpose, skills and talents, hobbies, and the best places for you to live or travel.

Q. How does healing occur?

A. Your Higher Self, also known as the Super-Consciousness, is able to effectively heal emotional

143

traumas from this life or earlier lives, to improve your self-confidence and self-esteem, and to help you set meaningful new goals.

Q. Will I be able to communicate with loved ones who have passed on?

A. Some clients communicate with loved ones and ancestors on the other side of the Veil, or experience other worlds or dimensions. Your Higher Self, Guides and the Light orchestrate your session and choose what is most beneficial and enjoyable for your unique journey.

Q. How long is a session? Will I experience a past life?

A. Initial sessions typically last three to five hours. Most – but not all – clients experience a past life or lives, and journey to the Spirit World. You will receive physical and emotional healing from the Light. We will review your questions for your Higher Self and Guides before your guided meditation so that Wendy may ask them on your behalf, and will debrief after your session to help anchor the healing and new insights.

Q. Will you record my session?

A. Yes. All sessions are recorded. You will learn more as you listen to your MP3 audio file, and need to follow your Higher Self's guidance to achieve lasting improvements in your health and well-being.

Note: Some clients vibrate above current recording capabilities during their session and the recording – or portions thereof – is blank, or filled with static. If this occurs, you will receive a session summary custom written report.

Q. May I schedule activities for the rest of the day after my session?

A. This is not recommended. Give yourself the gift of an unscheduled day to fully embrace your life-enhancing Regression Healing experience. You may want time to take a walk, nap, journal or draw. *Do NOT drive or conduct business for the remainder of the day.*

Q. When are sessions scheduled?

A. Sessions are typically scheduled on a Saturday or Sunday at 9 am Pacific Time/ noon Eastern, but there is some flexibility.

Contact Wendy at 425-502-0362 or via email at AuthorWendyRoseWilliams@hotmail.com to plan your date.

Q. Any recommendations before my session?

A. Meditate. Wendy can coach you how to get started if you haven't yet begun a meditation practice. Working with the 61-minute Regression Healing two-part guided meditation is highly recommended. You can use that MP3 audio file as many times as you like both before and after your personal Regression Healing™ session with Wendy.

Write a list of up to twenty questions regarding your health, wealth, relationships, career, life purpose and more for your Higher Self, Guides and the Light. We will also explore any karma and soul contracts requiring adjustment during your session.

Come with an open mind the day of your session, and release any expectations or concerns. Simply enjoy rediscovering the profound wisdom of your soul.

Q. Can sessions be done via Skype? Are they the same length and results?

A. Yes to both. A stable Skype connection from a laptop or PC (vs. Skype phone app) is required. You do not need a camera, as sessions require only a clear, reliable voice-to-voice connection.

Q. What if I don't have Skype or it's too complicated for me?

A. Sessions are also available via free conference calling. You simply call the phone number provided and enter the conference code at your appointed time. Regression Healing teleconference sessions are recorded as an MP3 audio file just as Regression Healing sessions are with Skype.

Q. Will I need more than one session?

A. There is no requirement or expectation of a follow-up session as sessions are quite comprehensive. Many clients need only one session, whereas others have a follow-up session 3-6 months or more later. Repeat clients are certainly welcome. Subsequent sessions tend to be much shorter (an average of two to two and a half hours) as you can reach a therapeutic level of trance quickly, and pick up right where you left off, even years later.

Q. Is Past-Life Regression suitable for everyone?

A. No. Regression Healing is contraindicated (should not be performed) for individuals with schizophrenia, who are bi-polar, or who have Dissociative Identity Disorder (DID).

Q. Do you offer Past Life Regression for children?

A. Wendy typically works with adults aged eighteen and older. If a younger child or teen needs healing, a session can be done with a parent or other adult they're close to as their surrogate. Alternatively, Wendy can refer you to a Past-Life Regressionist or other healer who works with children.

Wendy Rose Williams

REGRESSION HEALING TESTIMONIALS

"Wendy, you are medicine! You literally are medicine. That's what I got out of the regression, as well as my soul has lived many hard days all in preparation for this life. And this life is preparing me for the next. It really puts 'hard times' into perspective – like heat and pressure polish coal into a diamond. The hard times are necessary to improve my soul and to improve the world. I also realized how intertwined I am with the Civil War – the real start for the fight for true equality in the world. That is truly important to my soul, and wonderful guidance for me. Thank you for everything you do."

Jason Havey, Host "Spinning Logic" podcast (Austin, Texas)
JasonHavey.com

"My session was beyond amazing! Some of the information was astounding. There will be profound healing coming from this. I highly recommend Wendy as a Regression Healer, and will be sending clients to her."

Greg Baroni, Channel
(Shoreline, Washington)

Physical Healing

"I wanted to thank you once again, Wendy, for continually encouraging me. The Past-Life Regression was wonderful. My neck and back feel so much better! Bless you."

Lawrence Cenotto V, Author/ Playwright
"True North" travel adventure book series
(Shoreline, Washington)

"Wendy is nothing short of amazing. I was complaining to Facebook pals about a painful condition that kept me from riding my bicycle - not a minor problem for one whose primary transportation is a bike. Wendy asked me via Facebook private message if I wanted help with the issue and I said sure. She returned in a little while and told me that my pyramid is upside down. What pyramid? I didn't know I had a pyramid!

Wendy explained she was referring to the energy pattern associated with my chakras. Evidently all my energy was going to my upper body spiritual chakras and not enough was going to the lower chakras that connect me to Earth. This news, though I didn't fully understand it, did not surprise me. I've never felt very grounded and survival has always been a struggle for me.

Wendy offered to 'flip' my pyramid for me to help rebalance my energy to allow me to heal. I agreed. Within a few hours I felt the pain decreasing and powerful bursts of energy shooting into my legs and lower body. The next day I was able to take a brisk walk without feeling any of the lower back pain that usually accompanies such activity. Within a few days I was able to ride my bike again. I still don't understand what she did or how she did it but I'm feeling remarkably better, and Wendy did it!

Wendy suggested a past-life regression might help identify the source of my physical complaints. She was so patient. Wendy had to teach me how to Skype before I could avail myself of her service as we don't live in the same state. I made myself comfortable the day of my session, and Wendy talked me through a pleasant induction exercise and eventually brought me to a place where I could begin to observe my previous life.

The first thing Wendy told me to do was to look down at my feet and describe them to her. That was when things got weird. I could see only one foot. As I zoomed out and got a look at my whole person I discovered I was an old man with only one leg. And I was on a mission. I realized I must have been remarkably strong. I had just climbed a mountain on one leg and was about to start down the other side. I realized I was nearing the end of a long journey and also the end of my life. I had a crucial message – a pardon - to deliver. Once I placed it in the right hands, my life's work would be done.

As my present self watched my past self, I saw things that were bewildering to me and occasionally felt confused. When that happened, Wendy would ask me a question or give me an instruction that would clarify the situation and I would know what to do next. I walked through a temple that looked strikingly similar to my neighborhood movie theater. Wendy assured me it's not a problem to combine images from now with then. She encouraged me to keep moving and I stepped through a door into what would have been the theater parking lot except it was obviously just a small clearing in a dense forest. A man came out of the shadows to meet me and I knew he was the intended recipient of the letter I was carrying.

I wondered if I was making up stuff about the mountain trail and the weird lights and the temple that looked like a movie theater, but when the younger man, and the old man who was me, fell sobbing into each other's arms, I knew I wasn't making that up. I've never experienced anything like the emotion I felt as after half a lifetime, I delivered into his hands the pardon that would save my son's life.

Immediately after my session I discussed with Wendy what had happened. I did not make a clear connection between the young man and anyone in this life. It wasn't until days later that I realized that I had been a man who hobbled around on one leg for half his life. I realized that he probably had other damage to his lower body as well. I wondered if I was letting energy in this life leak out through the leg I was missing in that life. I didn't feel a miraculous healing take place as a result of recognizing the connection between that body and my current body. But that healing had already taken place a few days earlier when Wendy had flipped my pyramid and balanced my energy.

What I did feel was an enormous sense of relief and satisfaction at the completion of a task that had cost me everything, as it was worth it. It was some days later that I recognized the son in that past life in someone I know in this life. He is someone who came into my life recently, apparently with the purpose of bringing a message and with it the joy of a long-awaited reunion.

Donya Wicken, Author/ Playwright
(Sacramento, California)
TheZenofBen.com

Energy & Property Clearing

"I can't believe it! My large property improvement project (3+ years of energy blockage & delays), is finally underway! I put my faith and trust in Wendy's hands. Right after our session – (an all-new experience I didn't know what to make of, honestly) – immediately it was like this black cloud lifted! I cannot thank you enough for sharing your heart, soul, gifted talents & positive energy! THANK YOU for what you have done for our family."

JW, Real Estate Broker & Investor
(Kirkland, Washington)

Healing Anxiety & Depression

"Our session was an enlightening experience. It showed not only your talent, but how deeply passionate you are about bringing healing to people. Thank you!"
   K.P., Marketing Executive
   (Seattle, Washington)

"I've always been a little anxious about this kind of work. The gentle sound of Wendy's voice made it very easy for me to relax and before I knew it, I was recalling several past life memories with clear, concise details! I also got answers to questions I never thought were possible. I thoroughly enjoyed the journey."
   Rus Sullivan, Reiki Master/ Psychic Medium
   (Edmonds, Washington)
   DivinelyWrapped.com

"Wendy Williams is a highly gifted and powerful healer. Before the session even began, during the pre-amble, I could feel the energies in the room shifting and softening. At the time of my session, I was in a state of intense fear and was worried would I be able to relax and see any of my past lives.

I actually did see myself as a Shaman in the jungles of South America, but I was too afraid to go through with seeing that lifetime. Wendy was really patient with me, making necessary adjustments so that my experience would be positive and beneficial.

Our three- or so hour session was incredible!!!!!! I could not believe what I was seeing. The visualizations were stunningly real, and impacted me on a deep level emotionally. The last part of the session where we put light in different areas of the body was so deeply relaxing my initial fear diminished to practically zero. I would recommend her to the most skeptical of people. You will not be disappointed. Her work is exceptional."

Joel Henry, Astrologer & Dream Interpreter
(Arlington, Massachusetts)

"I went in to my regression session with Wendy with no expectations. I was dealing with a few things including looking for clarification on direction for some personal pursuits as well as some unresolved grief that had been weighing heavily on me for a number of years. The session was more than I could have imagined. Once it was over, I could feel a real change. It was like a weight had been lifted!

Emotionally, I feel back on track and I'm more focused on what I need to do to accomplish some of my goals. Wendy took the time to explain the process which really helped me and alleviated any hesitations I had. It's been a couple of months since my session but I can still feel the positive changes that took place. I highly recommend a session with her."

Jim Sullivan
(Edmonds, Washington)
LidoDeckVacations.com

"It is so helpful to see and feel what happened in a past life and how that influences, interferes, creates doubt and fears in this life. Once we see the reasons for our fears, it is easier to let them go. Wendy is very patient, has a soothing voice and knows the right questions to guide you to what you need to know. I am very grateful for her talent and services. It has helped me so much."

Valerie Shinn, Astrologer
(Redmond, Washington)
ValerieShinn.com

Attracting Financial Abundance

"I want to tell you more about the session I had with Wendy now that a few months have passed. I am in debt for her graciousness. I am not new to psychic work or readings or healings. I am a long-time practitioner. I know our abilities come from Spirit – we are just the hollow vessel. Therefore, I really treasure working with other healers, seeing their gifts and having spiritual experiences. This was much more than a past life regression. It was an in-depth, guided shamanic journey and spiritual tune-up. Wendy has my 'A-OK' for her ethical and thorough approach to energy work. There is preparation, and clear understanding what you are working on.

I was shown several lives I was not aware of. I was shown higher spiritual guides I had not tuned into, but am attracted to. The session cut past-life strings, something I just did not pay enough attention to, and do... again, Wendy is thorough. Since our session, things have been happening for me. Specifically resources I have sought for YEARS, have "fallen in my lap." And it just keeps getting better. I found legal help. I found help with my computer, and much more. I now seem to access all the right sources for things to happen in my life. There seems to be a synchronicity that has occurred. It is making a big difference in my life.

What is going on is the checklist of spiritual items she requested for me are all aligning. A big part of Spirit is you have to invite the help. They don't just come in and change your life. They respect your free will. You must ask for the help."

P.M., Shaman
(South Dakota)

Healing, Releasing & Celebrating Past Lives

"I can honestly say I am a changed person because of this session. I still have much to process, but wow... I have done taped regressions before, but this was different. I cannot say enough about how good Wendy is, how caring and how patient she was with me. It truly was one of the best experiences of my life. Thank you, Wendy, for being the awesome soul you are.

I suggest that before anyone does a live regression they first do several on-line ones so they are used to visualizing and accessing that part of the brain. I used to think that live regression isn't necessary, that doing on-line was enough. Truth is, at least in my case, I needed a live guide, and Wendy was the perfect choice. I am really feeling a lot better – this sounds weird, but I feel taller!"

Becky Buchko, Author
(Johnstown, Pennsylvania)

"I went in to my session without expectations, then walked away with the knowledge of a past life that is very meaningful and on point with what is happening currently in this lifetime. It helped so much to know why certain events/issues happen or keep reoccurring and, armed with that knowledge, I can begin the healing with releasing of that past life's energy. Wendy is very instrumental in the process. She is intuitively sensitive and knows how to word questions that assist in getting as definitive an answer as possible for her clients. I highly recommend Wendy, and would happily use her services again in the future."

Laurie Regan, Author and Intuitive Artist
(Seattle, Washington)

"I thoroughly enjoyed my session with Wendy, who has a smooth, soft, serene voice that is easy to follow. I also loved how Wendy can intuit the right questions to ask at the right time, as this enhanced my experience significantly. I highly recommend scheduling a session with Wendy, as she is a true natural when it comes to working with our spiritual essence. Thank you for making such an important and beautiful contribution to our lives, Wendy."

Angela Rose Pate
Quantum Healing Hypnotherapy Practitioner
(Kirkland, Washington)

"I want to take a minute to thank Wendy Williams for her help with the incredible Past-Life Regression she did for me. It has been several months now and looking back I can see how learning the why behind my obsession with the 1889 Johnstown Flood in some ways released me from that obsession and has healed a deep sorrow in my soul. I look forward to working with her again in the future, especially as I begin a new journey helping the victims tell their stories. May Spirit bless you, Wendy, for all that you do to help others along their spiritual path."

Becky Buchko, Author
(Johnstown, Pennsylvania)

Enhance Connection with Your Spiritual Guidance

"Had the most amazing regression healing with Wendy Williams. It was like a past-life regression on steroids, in a good way! Not only did I get insights into past lives needing to be released, but also got to talk with Aurora and other Higher Energies. I HIGHLY (can't say it enough) recommend this for anyone who needs spiritual/ physical healing, OR if you want to connect with the Higher Energies you work with, and to find out more about your mission. Wendy is absolutely amazing! I cannot tell you how freeing and uplifting this session was, truly incredible. I'm already planning another session."

Karen Downing, Soul Mission Facilitator
(Issaquah, Washington)
YourSoulMission.com

"I just experienced a wonderful past life regression with Wendy. To begin with, she prepared for the session in a very professional way. Wendy made sure she understood my questions and consulted with me to make sure they were asked in a positive, clear way, demonstrating an in-depth knowledge of spiritual work. Our session was wonderful. I was guided to make contact with past lives and she took me on a very in-depth guided tour covering many issues. I was taken to a deep meditative state and met Guides on a very high level that I did not know I had. Many answers came to me. Since my session I am much more at peace. Blocks and past life strings have been cut. I feel much more grounded and past hurts in my life no longer come up all the time. I am able to get right to work on things I want to be focusing on, and in a short amount of time have made incredible strides. Wendy offers a very in-depth guided journey that is wonderful and very productive. I highly recommend Wendy's work."

P.M., Shaman
(South Dakota)

Life Purpose & Career Clarity

"Wow. Just wow. This healing was incredible. It changes everything! You have a gift. It's very important you share this work with as many people as possible."

Tas Soul, Musician
(Issaquah, Washington)
reverbnation.com/tassoul

"Thanks so much for our session. You really helped me to move forward from all the chaos and take the next positive steps in my life. I have many deeper understandings of what's to come, and feel so much better! Blessings."

Kam, Student
(Germany)

"Wendy, I can't thank you enough for allowing me to have this opportunity. It has been something that I have wanted for a long time. It has given me clarity in my path and that is huge for me! It was a great experience, I felt totally safe in your hands and felt no judgment. You have a real talent for this, and it is something I hope you continue to share so other people benefit. You have a special gift!"

Mikie Woodruff, Reiki Master
(Everett, Washington)

"My regression healing with Wendy was so much more than I could have imagined! We viewed past lives that provided valuable insights, tools, and validation of my life path and career. I found the light healing to be extremely powerful. Wendy skillfully prompted me for additional information, which I found to be invaluable later when receiving answers to my questions. If you are considering past-life regression healing, contact Wendy. She is a warm and skilled professional."

Darcy Pariso, Psychic Medium
and Animal Communicator
(Shoreline, Washington)
DarcyPariso.com

Chakra Opening & Balancing

"If you are looking for a truly unique healing experience for the mind, body and soul, I would highly recommend a session with Wendy. I had a magnificent third-eye opening and yet incredibly grounding experience. I'm still feeling the healing effects days later, and I have no doubt this blissful state will continue for many months to come"!

Talitha Thompson
Co-Owner, Sundance Massage
(Kenmore, Washington)
SundanceMassage.com

Consciousness Expansion

"My session with Wendy was relaxing and expansive. I feel there is great benefit in the ability of this work to provide access to greater awareness of our nature as limitless and inter-dimensional beings."

Jude Ponton, DC, LAC
(Seattle, Washington)
Whispering-Dragon.com

BONUS EXCERPT FROM THE PREQUEL TO "THE FLOW: PLIMOTH PLANTATION," A METAPHYSICAL FICTION TRILOGY BY WENDY ROSE WILLIAMS

"Life is infinitely stranger than anything which the mind of man could invent."
   Mark Twain

From the Author's Note in the Prequel to "The Flow: Plimoth Plantation"

My world tipped sideways quite sharply two months after my incredible Life-Between-Lives spiritual regression session. I struggled to accept and then to address my own energetic issues that a dear friend outlined for me so gently yet powerfully during a pivotal phone call early in 2013.

A young female ghost had visited my friend Abby in her home and had not wanted to leave. Abby had to work hard to remove the heartbroken ghost, and didn't feel she had gone to the Light.

The surreal part was that ghost was ME from an earlier life I shared with Abby! How was this even possible? That disincarnated Earth-bound energy couldn't stay. She was causing serious disruptions to my current life, and now negatively impacting my friends. I had to help the heartbroken ghost. I had to help MYSELF. I had to get it together – quite literally. I didn't understand at the time I desperately needed a soul retrieval of that portion of my energy from the 1600s.

Who exactly was this heartbroken ghost? How could we BOTH be here at the same time? Why was she still here? What trauma had she endured during that early Colonial American life? Why wouldn't she go Home?

Ann Warren's ghost and I had to make peace. I needed to heal with this first of many soul retrievals. I had to raise my vibration, align with my Higher Self, and become sovereign in my own energy field.

My incredible journey to find, validate, learn from, heal and release and eventually celebrate an estimated sixty of my past lives suddenly escalated, all in the form of a broken-hearted ghost.

I was incredibly fortunate my first short story "A Tiny Bow and Arrow" was published in "The Spiritual Writers Network Best of 2014" collection January 2015. My "writer blueprint" was created with the publication of those five simple pages. It was becoming clear my life purpose included writing about waking up spiritually, reincarnation and past lives in order to help others.

I didn't write the following story in the traditional sense. It was more a matter of listening closely as Ann Warren Little told me her perspective of her life at the New Colony in the years 1623-1676. By the end of her long narrative, I finally understood why she didn't go Home for so long. I not only empathized with the source of her heartbreak, but more importantly knew how to heal her heart – my heart – how to get her Home to the Light, and how to integrate our energy, as we are the same soul.

Chapter I

My name was Anna Warren when my soul incarnated in the 1600s. I was always simply called Ann. I spent most of my life as an early settler or "First Comer" at Plimoth Plantation, also called "The New Colony." This area later became part of the Commonwealth of Massachusetts in the United States of America.

I was the second oldest of five daughters. Our father Richard Warren was a successful London grower and merchant. Our mother lived just long enough to birth five daughters like clockwork every two years between the years 1610-1618.

Sadly, my memories of Mother quickly faded as I was only six when she went Home. I would occasionally tell my three younger sisters charming stories about Mother upon request as it made them happy. I was not clear myself as the years rolled by if my stories were fact or fiction. If you tell a story the same way long enough, it takes on a life – a sustainable energy – of its own.

Richard Warren was born April twelfth, 1585 in Shoreditch, Middlesex, England. Father married Elizabeth Walker as his second wife on April 14, 1619. They married in Great Amwell in Hertfordshire, England.

My stepmother Elizabeth's father's name was Augustine. I don't recall her mother's name as it has been over three hundred years. Elizabeth is now my mother in present time, as my mother and stepmother at Plimoth switched roles in my current incarnation.

Elizabeth became an incredible mother to us over time. Once I was an adult – especially once I became a mother myself – I came to ever more admire and appreciate her immense sacrifice and kindness in not only taking care of another woman's five daughters as her own, but for truly loving, guiding, protecting and providing for us during her remarkably long life of ninety plus years. She seemed to love us as completely as the two sons she would later bear my father at the New Colony.

We appreciated her for so many reasons, including Elizabeth's incredible strength, intelligence, wisdom, and even temperament. Elizabeth Walker Warren stood out in a time when women blended in, and were most often only a reflection of their husbands and children.

Chapter II

Why did we choose to become Pilgrims and to journey from our comfortable life in England to such an uncertain future in the New World? In 1619 a law was passed in England making it illegal to discuss religion, even in private homes. This was enough oppression from the Crown that many chose to leave in search of religious freedom. Others left to seek greater financial fortune.

I remembered waving more and more sadly from the dock in 1620 when my father finally successfully departed aboard the Mayflower. I was nine years old when Father left for the New World. We were still waving with all our might when his ship had sailed completely out of sight. Perhaps we were afraid to stop waving as then he would truly be gone.

It was the Mayflower's third attempt to sail for America. The first was in July of 1620. Imagine going through the heart-wrenching emotions of saying goodbye and enduring that difficult parting not once, not twice, but three times! We all wondered *when* we would see Father again. We couldn't bear to think *if* we would see him again, which was more realistic.

As I thought back to my father's departure aboard the Mayflower on September sixth, 1620, Elizabeth had done a fine job comforting five extremely somber girls aged three to eleven. She distracted us with stories about what mischief the two dogs on board the Mayflower would create. We could see a huge English Bull Mastiff and a small Springer Spaniel running about on board that day, barking excitedly.

We later learned dogs are often taken aboard for long voyages to protect the food rations from rats. I was quite frightened at the thought of rats as they were not only nasty, but were thought to carry disease. Would the passengers be able to stay healthy?

A Bull Mastiff is a large and powerful dog that weighs as much as 110-130 pounds. They were originally bred to guard estates and are fiercely protective. We didn't realize at the time that the large Mastiff bitch was also being brought for protection in the New World, along with the guns and cannons. Those we could not miss seeing being loaded aboard the Mayflower. I understood guns were used in hunting, but cannons? What sort of place was this that Father was going to and where we would join him?

No one was willing to state aloud would Father be safe. Would we be safe and able to prosper alone in England without him? And what would happen when we went to join him in the New World? What would it really be like? Despite my young age, I knew there would be no turning back – this was a decision for a lifetime.

I heard adults describe the hundred-foot long Mayflower as a "typical merchant vessel of our day." I wasn't sure what that meant. I counted that she had at least six sails that I heard were adjustable – sailors either "put on" or "took off" more sail depending how much wind was available, and how rough or smooth the seas were. The grown-ups, especially the men, talked about her square-riggings, beaked bow, and high castle-like superstructures both front and back, which were called fore and aft. I heard those areas were to protect the cargo and crew in the worst weather. But what about the passengers – where would Father be?

The seamen boasted that the Mayflower's boxy shape and deep drag made her highly stable, but admitted beating against the wind could be painfully slow at times. A journey of three thousand miles would take several months as she wouldn't skim lightly over the seas. Therefore it would be a long time before we could hope for a letter from Father confirming he was safe in the New World.

The Mayflower passengers were to travel to a small settlement called Jamestowne where they would join a small number of our fellow Englishmen. Jamestowne – later Jamestown – would become part of the state of Virginia.

We would pray for Father's safety daily, both as a family, and on our own. Prayer was part of the fabric of our life. It provided comfort and clarity of thought, and was a way to express our gratitude to God.

Christopher Jones was the Ship's Master for Father's voyage. He was a part owner of the Mayflower ship. I didn't know what that implied other than I prayed he would take special care of his precious human cargo. Captain Jones was a highly experienced Ship's Master of approximately fifty years of age when he took Father and the other passengers aboard the Mayflower to the New World.

Ship's Masters later became known as Sea Captains. In our day the term "Sea Captain" was reserved specifically for the militia, but the word usage later broadened.

The Mayflower was rated at one hundred and eighty tons, which meant her hold would accommodate one hundred and eighty casks of wine. But what did that equate to in people? We could see what looked like more than a hundred people attempting to board the ship with Father. Would they all fit? How would they get along in such close quarters for months on end?

The Mayflower was classified as a "sweet ship" since the seamen said some of the wine inevitably spilled. They joked raucously the sweet aroma of the wine would help temper the stench of the bilge. I didn't understand what bilge was at the time.

I would learn three years later during my own perilous voyage aboard the Anne of London that bilge smells disgusting! It becomes increasingly vile the longer you are at sea. It was a horrific smell you couldn't escape except for a few precious moments topside. But we were down below deck in the cargo hold for most of the grueling journey, as were the Mayflower passengers. Be very clear the Mayflower class of ships were cargo ships, not passenger ships...

(to be continued)

The prequel to "The Flow: Plimoth Plantation" is expected to be available for sale on Amazon in early 2017 in both paperback and Kindle editions.

Email AuthorWendyRoseWilliams@hotmail.com if you'd like to be notified when it's available.

Wendy Rose Williams

AUTHOR CONTACT INFORMATION AND FREE SHORT STORY OFFER

Email: AuthorWendyRoseWilliams@hotmail.com

Phone/ Text: 425-502-0362

Facebook: Wendy Rose Williams

Skype: WendyRoseWilliams1234

Email AuthorWendyRoseWilliams@hotmail.com to receive a FREE copy of her short story "Ramona Falls: The Path to Forgiveness." This story was inspired by Wendy's past life pilgrimage to explore her past life as Jesse Applegate, the Oregon Wagon Train leader mentioned during Simon's Regression Healing session.

Your email address will be kept confidential and will not be sold or shared. You may receive occasional updates from the author such as requests for test readers, and notifications of new publications or courses Wendy will be teaching.

Bless you for your commitment to your own health and well-being as we heal the planet and the human race together through forgiveness and gratitude, and move into the Heaven on Earth energies of peace, love and joy.

"Love yourself first and everything else falls into line..."
Lucille Ball